Entrepreneurial Learning at Work

Entrepreneurial Learning at Work

Building People-First Ventures in a Changing World

Kathy Cowan Sahadath

BUSINESS EXPERT PRESS

Leader in applied, concise business books

Entrepreneurial Learning at Work:
Building People-First Ventures in a Changing World

Cover design by Cassandra Kronstedt

Interior design by S4Carlisle Publishing Services, Chennai, India

First published in 2026 by
Business Expert Press, LLC
222 East 46th Street, New York, NY 10017
www.businessexpertpress.com

ISBN-13: 978-1-63742-946-4 (paperback)
ISBN-13: 978-1-63742-947-1 (e-book)

Entrepreneurship and Small Business Management Collection

First edition: 2026
10 9 8 7 6 5 4 3 2 1

EU SAFETY REPRESENTATIVE
Mare Nostrum Group B.V.
Mauritskade 21D
1091 GC Amsterdam
The Netherlands
gpsr@mare-nostrum.co.uk

Description

Entrepreneurial Learning at Work: Building People-First Ventures in a Changing World is not another "growth hack" manual or start-up playbook. Where most entrepreneurship books focus on scaling fast, raising capital, or chasing disruption, this book reframes entrepreneurship as a reflective, relational, and human-centered practice.

It offers a different lens: ventures as living systems that grow when people grow. Through real-world founder stories, practical tools, and research distilled into plain language, readers learn how to design ventures that are resilient, inclusive, and future ready, ventures that thrive not just because of strategy but because of the integrity and adaptability of the people who lead them.

Entrepreneurial Learning at Work speaks to founders, builders, team leaders, small business owners, and entrepreneurial educators who believe businesses thrive when people do. This is not a book about scaling faster or hustling harder. It's about building ventures as living systems: reflective, resilient, and rooted in purpose.

Through vivid founder stories, accessible tools, and people-first practices, you'll learn how to:

- Turn everyday experiences into learning practices that fuel innovation.
- Design workplaces where diverse identities and voices thrive.
- Grow talent from within, passing the torch without losing values.
- Navigate transitions, burnout, exits, succession, with renewal.
- Make learning visible and scalable in hybrid, digital-first teams.

Ready to build a business that people love working for, and customers love buying from? This book is your blueprint for mastering the human side of entrepreneurship. Whether you're hiring your first employee or leading a growing team, you'll discover practical strategies to attract top talent, foster a resilient culture, and lead with clarity and heart.

Don't just build a company. Build a venture by growing your people, your culture, your own leadership. Turn the page … and start leading like the founder your team deserves.

Contents

List of Tables

Introduction: Rethinking Entrepreneurship as Learning Leadership

A Different Kind of Entrepreneurship Book

Most shelves on entrepreneurship look the same. They promise speed, scale, and the secrets of start-up unicorns. These books often speak to boardrooms and pitch decks—not to entrepreneurs leading through people, purpose, and day-to-day learning. This book is written for those growing real ventures in the real world: trades-based founders, community-rooted builders, professional service entrepreneurs, and those navigating reinvention. Whether you're building from the ground up or adapting an existing business to meet today's shifting demands, this book offers a grounded, people-first path forward.

But if you're picking up this book, chances are you're asking different questions. You're not only wondering, How do I grow the business? You're also wondering:

- How do I grow people while I grow the business?
- How do I make my venture reflect my values?
- How can I lead in a way that feels human and sustainable?

This book is meant for founders, builders, team leaders, and entrepreneurial educators who believe businesses thrive when people do. It's not about shortcuts or hacks. It's about building ventures as living systems, adaptive, reflective, and designed with people at the center.

Not Just Any Leader

While many of the tools in this book are grounded in leadership and adult learning theory, this book is unapologetically written for people building something of their own. Entrepreneurs face unique pressures: identity shifts, emotional risk, uneven resources, and personal accountability. This lens shapes every chapter.

A Story to Begin

When Rosa launched her landscaping business, she thought success would come from skill, speed, and hard work. And in the early days, it did. She managed every client relationship, solved every problem, and made sure the work met her standards.

But growth brought new challenges. Each season, she hired more people, but the questions never stopped flowing back to her. Crew members repeated the same mistakes. Training was inconsistent. Rosa felt she was running harder every year but not moving forward.

Finally, she tried something different. Instead of fixing every problem herself, she started building simple learning rituals. Weekly "what worked/what didn't" check-ins. Pairing new hires with mentors. Celebrating mistakes that turned into lessons.

Her business didn't just grow in revenue. It grew in resilience. She had more time, her team had more confidence, and clients noticed the professionalism. The turning point wasn't a new marketing tactic or pricing model. It was learning, made visible, shared, and scaled across her venture.

This book is about those turning points. The moments when entrepreneurs stop running harder and start building systems that grow with them.

Why This Book, Why Now

The world of work is shifting. Millennials and Gen Z make up more of the workforce each year. They expect autonomy, flexibility, inclusion, and purpose (Deloitte 2025). Remote and hybrid realities are no longer exceptions but norms. Diversity and inclusive leadership are no longer "nice to haves" they are requirements for resilience and relevance (Katsaros 2024).

In Canada and globally, platforms like MaRS Discovery District now deliver entrepreneurial support entirely online, showing how learning ecosystems can stretch from coast to coast (MaRS 2023). Entrepreneurs are no longer just building businesses; they're designing the future of work.

And yet, too many entrepreneurship books still frame ventures as machines: input the right strategy, output profit. This book sees ventures as living systems: adaptive, human, and reflective.

What You'll Find Here

This book offers three things you won't find together anywhere else:

1. **Life Course Lens**
   - Entrepreneurship as a developmental journey across career transitions, caregiving, reinvention, burnout, and succession
   - This is not just about start-ups; it's about ventures evolving across a lifetime.
2. **Practice, Pedagogy, and Purpose**
   - Each chapter blends practical tools, learning design, and values-driven reflection.
   - This integration helps you not only solve problems but embed learning into your systems.
3. **People-First, Inclusive Approach**
   - Instead of focusing on hustle or investor ROI, we center resilience, psychological safety, and inclusive leadership as the engines of sustainable growth.

The Personas: Who This Book Is For

To guide the journey, you'll meet five composite personas drawn from real-world founders and entrepreneurs:

- **The Purpose-Driven Founder** who left corporate life to build a consultancy anchored in ethics and empathy
- **The Builder-Coach** a trades-based entrepreneur ready to pass the torch and grow leadership in his crew
- **The Emerging People Leader** promoted into leadership at a nonprofit, balancing burnout and potential

- **The Reflective Entrepreneurial Educator** who is teaching and coaching entrepreneurship, seeking tools that blend research and practice
- **The Social Entrepreneur or Maker-Founder** weaving life, community, and creativity into ventures that must scale without losing soul

These personas reappear through stories, examples, and prompts. They are mirrors for you, the reader, to see your own journey reflected in theirs.

How the Book Works

Each chapter follows a consistent rhythm:

- **Turning Point Opening Narrative**—a founder's real turning point
- **Core Concepts**—research translated into plain, actionable insights
- **Founder Spotlights or Profiles**—extended case studies of entrepreneurs leading with reflection and resilience
- **Visual Tool**—simple, usable frameworks (maps, trackers, canvases) you can apply for yourself or with your team
- **Talk About It with Your Team**—prompts for dialogue and collective learning
- **Chapter Close and Transition**—a transition to carry the theme forward.
- **A Word of Encouragement**—short motivational quotes designed to meet you where you are

This rhythm ensures the book is not only read but used.

What Makes This Book Different

This book stands apart because it reframes entrepreneurship as a learning journey, one built on systems, relationships, values, and the honest realities of growth.

- **Not just strategies but systems.** We don't just tell you what to do; we show you how to build learning into your culture.
- **Not just solo hustle but shared growth.** We frame entrepreneurship as collective and relational, not just individual.
- **Not just scaling fast but scaling wisely.** We care about legacy, sustainability, and alignment with values.
- **Not just success stories but struggles and learning.** Every founder spotlight includes mistakes, doubts, and recovery.

An Invitation

This is a book about entrepreneurship. But it's also about leadership, identity, and growth. It's about building ventures that not only withstand uncertainty but grow because of it. Because learning isn't just a tool in your entrepreneurial toolkit, it's the foundation.

As you move through the chapters, take your time. Pause often. Try the tools. Share the prompts with your team, your mentors, or your peers. Let the stories spark moments of reflection. You don't need to take it all in at once. Instead, treat your venture for what it already is: a living system. Your business is not just what you offer; it's how you choose to grow, adapt, and lead.

Throughout this book, you'll encounter reflective tools, leadership models, conversational frameworks, and practices you can apply right away, or return to as your context shifts. These are not prescriptions. They're invitations. Take what speaks to your current reality. Set aside what doesn't resonate, at least for now. Some pieces may offer clarity, others might challenge your assumptions or affirm what you've already known deep down.

Above all, this is not about getting it perfect. It's about being present, staying curious, and leading with purpose. Whether you're just starting, evolving in place, or navigating a significant transition, this book is here to support the path you're already walking, as a learning leader, a people-centered builder, and someone creating a business that reflects what matters most.

Too often, entrepreneurial books center strategy, growth hacks, or founder hustle. This book is different. It focuses on learning as a leadership practice, one that helps entrepreneurs build ventures where people, identity, and purpose evolve together. Grounded in stories from real-world founders and backed by learning theory, it repositions entrepreneurship as an adaptive, reflective journey—not just a business model.

"Entrepreneurs don't just build companies. They build the conditions in which people learn, grow, and thrive."

What You'll Find Along the Way

As you move through the chapters of this book, you'll notice short motivational quotes designed to meet you where you are, whether you're sketching out your first business plan at your kitchen table, expanding a family-run operation, or adapting an established venture to today's changing work environment.

These reflections aren't just inspirational; they're practical reminders that entrepreneurship is not a one-size-fits-all path. Each quote is here to anchor your mindset, offer a pause, and remind you why your work matters.

We've chosen words that resonate with real-world founders: the entrepreneurs in motion, in transition, in reflection. Those in trades, tech, creative industries, professional services, community-rooted businesses, and all those who've carved out their own path.

You may find a quote that sticks with you. Revisit it. Mark it. Share it. Let it nudge you forward. Because your business isn't just what you do, it's how you grow.

About the Stories in This Book

Over years of teaching, coaching, and walking alongside founders, I've seen the power of reflection not just as a tool but as a lifeline. This book offers a way of seeing your work, your learning, and your people through a more intentional lens. I hope it helps you grow with integrity, and on your own terms. The entrepreneur profiles and founder spotlights throughout this book reflect the real experiences of people building ventures across industries, communities, and life stages. Their stories were gathered through interviews, observations, and reflective conversations. While the insights and journeys are true to life, names and some identifying details have been changed, but the experiences, lessons, and insights are authentically theirs.

Acknowledgments

This book would not have been possible without the support, insight, and encouragement of many people along the way.

To my family, friends, and colleagues and collaborators (past and present), thank you for the engaging conversations, thoughtful feedback, and shared commitment to meaningful leadership. Your contributions helped shape the ideas and tools in these pages. To the entrepreneurs and teams I've had the privilege of working with, your courage, curiosity, and honesty in navigating and building your businesses inspired much of what this book explores. The real-world experiences you shared gave life to theory and grounded every chapter in practice.

To the editorial and publishing team, your guidance, professionalism, and attention to detail brought this vision to life. I'm deeply grateful for your partnership. And to the readers, thank you for investing your time and trust. I hope this book becomes a helpful companion in your leadership journey, sparking reflection, dialogue, and meaningful change.

To my greatest supporters, my late husband Cyril, and my brilliant son Casey, thank you for believing in me. Your presence, perspective, and questions have stayed with me and continue to shape how I move through the world.

Review Quotes

"Reading this book felt like finally hearing my story told with the respect and depth it deserves. As someone who learned by doing, mentoring, and adapting on the fly, I appreciated how it didn't glorify flashy start-ups, but celebrated everyday innovation. The tools are practical; the stories are real. I'll be using this with my apprentices and in my own planning."—**Master Plumber and Business Owner**

"This book doesn't just speak to entrepreneurs; it listens to us. As an artist navigating both identity and enterprise, I felt affirmed by its inclusive language and flexible approach. It gave me a framework for honoring my cultural roots while building a sustainable business rooted in values."—**Textile Artist and Workshop Facilitator**

"I didn't expect to see myself in a book like this, but I did, and that meant everything. The way it captures learning in motion, and how it values lived experience, helped me recognize myself as a real entrepreneur."—**Founder of Mobile Bike Repair**

"As someone who ran a small community business for over two decades, this book stirred memories and offered fresh insight, proof that learning doesn't end when you hand over the keys. I saw my younger self in many of the pages: figuring things out as I went, building relationships, and shaping a space that mattered to people. What I love most is how it affirms the slow wisdom of experience alongside today's fast-paced world. I'd recommend it to anyone starting out, but also to those of us reflecting on the meaning of what we built."—**Former Owner of a Lakeside Bookshop and Café**

PART 1

Building the Learning-Centered Venture

CHAPTER 1

Before We Begin: Seeing Your Venture as a Living Journey

Turning Point Opening Narrative: From Antiques to Candles

When KJ opened her antique shop, she thought it would be the business she ran for life. She loved restoring furniture, sourcing pieces, and helping people bring history into their homes. But a few years in, her priorities shifted. Her children were young, money was tight, and the store's long hours no longer fit her life.

One holiday season, she experimented with something small, hand-poured candles made in her kitchen. Customers loved them. Soon, the candles outsold the antiques. KJ hesitated. Was she abandoning her vision? Or was her vision evolving?

She chose to evolve. Over time, her antique shop became a candle and home goods studio. The core purpose, bringing beauty and meaning into people's lives, was still there. But the form changed to meet both her family's needs and her clients' tastes.

KJ's story reminds us: Entrepreneurship is not static. It's a journey shaped by the twists and turns of life.

Core Concepts

1. **Entrepreneurial Identity Evolves Over Time**
   Entrepreneurs aren't "born." They're shaped by transitions: career pivots, family roles, setbacks, and community ties. Every turning point adds another layer to who you are as a leader.
   Practical takeaway: Reflect on the turning points that have most influenced how you lead today.

2. **Vision Is Not Just Strategy—It's a Lifelong Narrative**
A vision isn't a one-time business plan. It's an evolving story of where you've been, what you value, and what you aspire to. Filion (2023) calls these *"emerging visions,"* visions that adapt over time.
   Practical takeaway: Map how your business vision has shifted alongside life changes, and notice what values have stayed constant.

3. **Entrepreneurial Learning Is Lifelong and Nonlinear**
Most of your real lessons come from doing, failing, reflecting, and adapting. Books and courses help, but your growth comes from lived moments.
   Practical takeaway: Treat mistakes and pivots as part of your curriculum.

4. **Balancing Personal and Professional Roles Is Central**
Entrepreneurship isn't separate from life, it's woven through family responsibilities, caregiving, and personal health. Sociologists call this linked lives: Our business choices are connected to the lives around us.
   Practical takeaway: Notice how family, friends, and community shape your entrepreneurial path.

5. **Context Matters: Time, Place, and Social Change Shape Ventures**
Entrepreneurs aren't just responding to markets. They're navigating history, culture, and economy. For example, a venture in 2025 is shaped by hybrid work, social change, and global uncertainty in ways it wasn't 20 years ago.
   Practical takeaway: Step back and ask, What broader forces are shaping my decisions right now?

6. **Cumulative Advantage and Disadvantage**
Some start with role models, financial cushions, or networks. Others face barriers rooted in culture, gender, or access. These early conditions matter, but they don't define your future.
   Practical takeaway: Reflect: What advantages or barriers shaped your path, and how can you leverage or counter them now?

7. **Intrapreneurs Are Entrepreneurs, Too**

Entrepreneurship doesn't only happen in start-ups. Intrapreneurs, those driving change within organizations, share the same mindset of reflection, experimentation, and purpose.

Practical takeaway: Even if you're not "the founder," you're still shaping systems, people, and culture.

Founder Spotlight: Vision in Transition—From Antique Shop to Candle Studio

KJ's story is about adapting vision, not abandoning it. Her values stayed constant, bringing meaning and beauty into daily life. But the expression shifted as her family grew and customer needs changed.

Her lesson: Vision evolves with life. Sustainable entrepreneurs don't cling to one fixed picture. They grow into new ones.

Vision and Identity Map

Use this map to trace how your entrepreneurial vision has evolved across your life course (Table 1.1).

How to use it: Fill in your turning points. Notice patterns. Share with your team as a way to explain why you lead the way you do.

Table 1.1 Vision and identity map

Stage	Turning point	What shifted in my vision?	What values stayed constant?
Early Life/Influences	Family expectations, role models	Belief in independence, work ethic	Integrity, creativity
Early Career/Start-Up	First venture, job changes	From independence → team building	Growth, adaptability
Mid-Career/Transition	Parenthood, caregiving, pivots	From scale → balance	Purpose, trust
Current Stage	Today's venture reality	Emerging vision for next chapter	Values that anchor me

Talk About It with Your Team

Use these questions to spark meaningful team conversations that connect personal experience with how you build, lead, and grow together.

- What life experiences shaped the way I lead today?
- How has our team's vision shifted alongside changes in our lives?
- What values keep showing up, no matter what changes?
- How can we support each other in balancing life and business?

Chapter Close and Transition

Entrepreneurship is not just about markets or models. It's about people growing over time. Seeing your venture through a life course lens helps you connect dots that might otherwise feel scattered: your past lessons, your present challenges, your future aspirations.

This book will keep returning to that lens, in founder stories, in tools, and in prompts that ask you not just how you're building your business but how your business is building you.

"Before we dive in, pause to see your venture not just as a project, but as part of your evolving life story."

CHAPTER 2

Beyond the Start-Up Myth

Entrepreneurship as an evolving leadership identity, not just launching a business but growing people, purpose, and adaptability.

Turning Point Opening Narrative: The Café Decision

The rain hit the sidewalk with rhythmic force as Mira stared at her laptop, untouched cappuccino cooling beside her. She wasn't a "start-up founder," not in the way the articles talked about. No accelerators, no seed capital, no hoodie-and-headphones aesthetic—just a quiet idea born out of necessity: She wanted to create space for caregivers like her, who needed flexible work and real understanding.

Two years in, the business was steady, but she felt stuck. Growth meant hiring. Hiring meant leadership. Leadership meant … becoming someone she wasn't sure she was ready to be.

Across from her sat Jamie, an early customer-turned-friend. "What you've created matters," Jamie said. "But it can't just be your hustle forever. The real work now is building something that others can grow with."

Mira closed her laptop slowly. Maybe it was time to stop seeing herself as a freelancer with a vision, and start seeing herself as a leader with a venture.

The story above reflects more than a personal pivot; it captures the quiet resilience and intentional leadership at the heart of entrepreneurial learning. As we move into this chapter's core concepts, we'll explore how entrepreneurship is not just a job but a deeply personal choice. It means staking your time, identity, and often your financial stability on something uncertain. Unlike managers or employees, entrepreneurs often build without safety nets, facing high risk, personal doubt, and constant decisions that affect others. This book speaks directly to those experiences. Building a venture in today's shifting world calls for more than strategy; it demands clarity of purpose, adaptability, and a deep investment in the growth of both the founder and the team. This chapter unpacks these foundational ideas, offering a new lens on what it means to lead a learning-centered, people-first business.

Core Concepts

1. **The Start-Up Myth Versus the Entrepreneurial Reality**
   Mainstream portrayals of entrepreneurship focus on rapid growth, tech disruption, and funding rounds. But most entrepreneurs, especially those building people-first ventures, navigate quiet, complex realities. These ventures evolve through purpose, people, and practice, not hype.

2. **Entrepreneurship as Leadership**
   Entrepreneurship is not just about product–market fit; it's about people–practice fit. Founders grow into leaders by making decisions that shape not just what their business does, but how it learns, adapts, and includes.

3. **Identity and Life Course**
   Entrepreneurial identity evolves over time, through transitions like career shifts, family changes, burnout, renewal, and growth. Entrepreneurs often redefine themselves alongside their businesses, navigating changing priorities and life stages.

4. **Work as a Learning System**
   People-first ventures thrive when learning is integrated into daily work. Entrepreneurial leadership means designing cultures where experimentation, feedback, and personal development are part of the rhythm, not left to chance.

> *"You don't have to be the loudest in the room to build something that matters."*

Reframing Entrepreneurship Through a Life Course Lens

Entrepreneurial Learning at Work reframes entrepreneurship as a learning practice over the life course—not just a phase in launching a business. This book speaks directly to those who lead from the frontlines—entrepreneurial leaders who are building businesses, mentoring teams, juggling competing roles, and growing personally while navigating economic uncertainty, talent shifts, and deep societal change.

When we speak of the life course in this context, we're acknowledging that entrepreneurship is not a one-time event but an evolving identity shaped by lived experience, personal transitions, and shifting values (Corley and Miller 2005; Cowan Sahadath 2009). Entrepreneurs bring their whole selves to their ventures: their upbringing, setbacks, career pivots, family dynamics, and aspirations for the future. These elements influence not just what they build but how they lead, make decisions, and adapt. A life course lens surfaces the developmental, emotional, and relational dimensions of entrepreneurial leadership, often overlooked, yet critical to sustainable success.

Entrepreneurship doesn't happen in a vacuum. It unfolds across a life—shaped by childhood lessons, career twists, caregiving responsibilities, financial stress, aging parents, and the deep desire to build something meaningful. This book embraces that reality.

We call it a life course lens: a way of seeing your venture and your leadership not just as a job or a phase but as part of a longer, evolving journey. Whether you're in your 20s imagining what's possible, in your 40s balancing growth with purpose, or in your 60s thinking about legacy, you are still learning and adapting.

This lens shows up throughout the book:

- In **founder stories** that highlight personal crossroads and resilience
- In **tools** that help you reflect on more than just quarterly targets
- In **practices** that respect how your identity, energy, and priorities shift over time

We're not just building businesses; we're building lives around them. And when we pause to reflect on the full arc of our experience, we become better entrepreneurs, collaborators, and mentors.

"You don't just grow your business; you grow with it."

Unlike traditional start-up guides that focus on growth hacking or investment pitches, this book is grounded in real stories from entrepreneurs who are doing the slower, often unseen work of shaping inclusive cultures, nurturing talent, navigating personal transitions, and leading reflectively.

Through these stories, and the profiles woven throughout, we explore how entrepreneurial learning happens: in the moments of struggle, adaptation, mentorship, and meaning-making. You'll meet a business owner who transformed her financial services business into an intergenerational learning hub; a tree care leader who built a thriving team through a safety-first culture; and a founder who recalibrated her identity when a life change redirected her business entirely. Their stories illustrate how every entrepreneurial journey is also a leadership journey, one shaped by feedback, relationships, and evolving purpose.

Each chapter is built around the **Three Anchors** that shape entrepreneurial learning:

- **Practice**—the daily habits, tools, and leadership behaviors that support growth
- **Pedagogy (instruction)**—the way we design learning into work: mentorship, feedback, peer discussions, and reflective conversations
- **Purpose**—the values and mission that guide decision making and provide resilience through change

This book is for entrepreneurial leaders who grow businesses and people with care and intention—curious, reflective, and purpose-driven venture architects shaping the future of work, one decision at a time.

You can read it solo or with your team. Each chapter includes:

- A turning point opening narrative
- A founder profile highlighting lived complexity
- A visual tool or practice to apply in your business
- Reflective prompts and team conversation starters
  We're not chasing hustle here. We're cultivating learning, because it's how we build ventures that last, cultures that matter, and people who thrive.

Founder Spotlight: A Financial Planner's Pivot Toward Purpose

This entrepreneur began her career in the insurance industry in the late 1980s, later stepping away to raise children before returning to the financial services field in the early 1990s. Upon rejoining the profession, she joined forces with her mother and eventually took over her retirement planning business. What began as a continuation of a family legacy became a deeply personal and evolving journey of entrepreneurial leadership.

Working across Canadian provinces, she offers retirement and estate planning services through a range of financial products, from mutual funds to segregated investments and executor services. Her approach reflects not just technical expertise but a values-driven practice grounded in empathy, legacy, and trust. As her client base aged, she adapted by acquiring various certifications and designations to better support clients navigating aging and loss, underscoring her commitment to relational leadership in business.

Over time, she expanded her influence beyond her business through active community involvement, notably with a long-standing service club, where she held leadership roles and earned recognition for her contributions.

Her story reflects a model of entrepreneurship not built on disruption, but on care, adaptability, and purposeful transition. By growing herself alongside her business, and remaining attuned to her clients' changing needs, she exemplifies the quiet, people-centered evolution of entrepreneurial leadership in a changing world.

Entrepreneur Profile Snapshot

Business Name: Financial Services Venture

Industry: Financial Planning and Estate Services

Years in Operation: 30+ years (with transitions and generational continuity)

Location: Multiple provinces in Canada

Turning Point

The entrepreneur transitioned from raising a family back into financial services, taking over her mother's retirement planning business. A major turning point came when she responded to the evolving needs of aging clients by earning advanced designations in the field.

Core Learning

Leadership is relational and responsive. The entrepreneur demonstrated that trust, adaptability, and community service form the core of people-first entrepreneurship. She grew the business by staying close to client needs and leading with empathy.

Theme Tie-In

This story exemplifies a shift from individual contribution to venture leadership. Rather than chasing scale or disruption, the business grew by honoring values, legacy, and human-centered service.

Life Course Reflection

The entrepreneur's journey was shaped by intergenerational transition, caregiving responsibilities, and a return to professional work after parenting. Her life course deeply influenced the evolution of the business and her identity as a leader.

Quote

Sometimes the most important investment isn't financial, it's showing up for people when they need you most.

The journey you've just read highlights how personal transitions, parenting, caregiving, career shifts, and generational influence, shape not only the entrepreneur's identity but also the evolution of their business. These inflection points are not detours; they are part of the entrepreneurial path. To help you reflect on your own trajectory, and the experiences that continue to inform your decisions, we introduce the Life Course Reflection Canvas. This tool invites you to step back and consider how your personal history, social context, and evolving purpose influence your leadership today and into the future.

The Life Course Reflection Canvas: Connecting Identity, Experience, and Entrepreneurial Leadership

The Life Course Reflection Canvas is more than a self-assessment; it's a structured opportunity for founders to make visible the invisible threads that shape their leadership. In a world where entrepreneurship is often equated with speed, scale, or market disruption, this tool slows the pace and turns attention inward, toward the lived experiences, turning points, and personal values that form the true architecture of people-first ventures.

This canvas invites entrepreneurs to map key stages of their life and work, highlighting formative transitions, identity shifts, personal responsibilities, and moments of clarity or uncertainty. By reflecting on how these events have influenced your leadership decisions, team dynamics, and venture direction, you build not only self-awareness but also strategic clarity.

Why It Matters

Chapter 2 reframes entrepreneurship not as a fixed identity but as an evolving leadership practice, rooted in people, purpose, and adaptation. The Life Course Reflection Canvas brings this idea to life by showing how every founder's path is shaped by more than business strategy. From returning to work after caregiving, to navigating loss or opportunity, the decisions entrepreneurs make are human first, and those stories shape the cultures they create.

How It Supports the Purpose of This Book

The broader aim of *Entrepreneurial Learning at Work* is to help entrepreneurs and small business owners grow resilient, learning-centered organizations by investing in themselves and their people. This tool supports that aim by encouraging intentional reflection and helping entrepreneurs connect the dots between personal growth and organizational evolution. When we understand where we've been, we are better equipped to build what comes next, with empathy, integrity, and courage.

Tool: The Life Course Reflection Canvas

It is a visual/journaling tool that invites readers to consider:

- What transitions shaped your entrepreneurial path?
- How has your definition of "success" changed over time?
- What values or social issues are emerging as part of your purpose?
- What type of leadership are you growing into?

Reflection Prompt (Individual or Team Use):

When did you stop seeing yourself as an individual contributor, and begin thinking like a leader of people, culture, and change?

Three Anchors in Action—Bringing Strategy, Culture, and Growth Together

In this section, we ground each chapter's big ideas in what actually drives entrepreneurial success day to day. These "anchors" are the core elements that help business owners not just survive but lead with clarity and impact, even in a changing world:

- **Practice**
  This is the leadership habits, systems, and tools you put in place to run your business and guide your team. These are the repeatable actions that build momentum, from how you hold meetings to how you give feedback, delegate work, or learn from your customers.
- **People and Learning** (aka Pedagogy and Instruction)
  This is the way you grow talent, share knowledge, and build a culture where people can learn on the job. Whether it's peer mentoring, coaching conversations, tailgates, or onboarding new team members, this anchor turns your business into a place where growth is part of the work.

- **Purpose**

  The values, mission, and vision that drive your decisions and keep your business aligned. This anchor is about staying connected to why you do what you do, and how that purpose shapes not only your leadership but the way your team shows up and your business evolves.

Together, these anchors help you build a business that's not just operationally sound but human centered, resilient, and future ready.

Talk About It with Your Team

At the close of Chapter 2, I encourage you to reflect on these questions to connect the personal lens of the entrepreneur with the shared journey of the business.

- Where do you see purpose shaping your business decisions right now?
- What life experiences shaped the way you work?
- Is your team clear on why we're building this business the way you are?
- How can you bring more intentionality to how you grow, ourselves and others?

This turns the tool into a team tool. It opens up meaningful conversations about purpose, culture, and personal growth, which are critical in the early stages of any business and throughout ongoing reinvention.

Signature Practice: Life Course Reflection Canvas

Use the Tool: As you reflect on your entrepreneurial path and prepare for the future, use the Life Course Reflection Canvas to map pivotal experiences, shifts in identity, and turning points in purpose. This tool helps you translate your personal journey into business clarity, and is designed to grow with you.

Business owners want tools they can use, not just ideas they can read about. The Life Course Reflection Canvas helps entrepreneurs visualize their development and reconnect with why they started. It's perfect for revisiting annually or during strategic planning sessions.

As you reflect on your journey so far, your identity, your story, your shifting sense of purpose, remember that these are not distractions from building a business. They are the foundation of it. In today's dynamic economy, it's not just the venture that must evolve. The entrepreneur must, too. What you choose to learn, unlearn, or reimagine at this stage will shape every decision you make going forward. And that's where we go next: stepping fully into your role as a learner, one who grows not just the business but the people within it.

Chapter Close and Transition

You don't need to be the perfect founder. You just need to keep learning. Chapter 3 explores how real entrepreneurs integrate reflection into their everyday decision making, not as a side activity but as a tool for survival, clarity, and continuous reinvention.

What does it mean to lead a business while still learning who you are? How can reflection be a strategic tool, not just a soft skill?

- Chapter 3 explores the mindset of the entrepreneurial learner and introduces the learning cycle: try it → think about it → make it better

Entrepreneurship is one big experiment. You don't need to have everything figured out; you just need to stay in motion.

Here's how learning really works in a growing business:

- **Try It**—You take action. Launch the offer. Hire the person. Test the idea.
- **Think About It**—You pause. What worked? What didn't? What surprised you?
- **Make It Better**—You adjust. Tweak the process. Change the plan. Try again, smarter.

This is how progress happens in real life, not from perfect plans, but from learning in motion. Use this cycle often. Build it into your meetings, your team check-ins, your own routines (Table 2.1).

Table 2.1 The learning cycle

Step	What it means	Real-world example
Try It	Take action. Launch the idea. Test the service. Hire the person.	You try a new pricing model or pilot a new product line.
Think About It	Reflect on what happened. What worked? What didn't?	Sales dipped. Customers asked more questions than expected.
Make It Better	Adjust your approach based on what you've learned.	You revise the offer, improve your pitch, and simplify the pricing.

Use this Weekly or Monthly

This isn't a one-time tool. It's a habit. You can use it:

- In your team huddles
- During project debriefs
- In your personal journaling
- After customer interactions

This is how progress happens, not from perfect plans, but from purposeful practice. In Chapter 3, we'll look at how to apply this cycle to your daily work, team rhythms, and long-term goals. Reflection is more than a soft skill, it's a strategic advantage. Let's start learning forward.

The Entrepreneur as Learner: Navigating Growth Across the Life Course

We don't just grow businesses. We grow into the kind of people who can lead them.

Turning Point Opening Narrative: Chloe's Turning Point

Chloe wiped down the last counter of the café she had managed for years, the quiet hum of the espresso machine fading behind her. It was closing time, and she was exhausted. She had spent the past decade in hospitality, long shifts, constant motion, and little time for reflection. She was good at what she did, but the work no longer fit her life.

When she finally stepped away, it was less a master plan than a leap into the unknown. She wanted something of her own, something slower, something that could flex with her new role as a mother. She started small, handcrafting skincare products in her kitchen. What began as curiosity turned into demand. Friends asked for more. Local markets sold out. Suddenly she was an entrepreneur.

But growth came with weight. For the first year, she did everything herself, formulating, producing, packaging, selling. Late nights blurred into early mornings. Burnout loomed. She snapped at her partner, forgot appointments, and asked herself, *"Am I really cut out for this?"*

The breaking point came one winter. Orders piled up, her child was sick, and she nearly walked away. Instead, she tried something different: She delegated. She hired part-time help and began reflecting weekly on what was working, and what wasn't. Slowly, the pressure eased. Her team grew, her confidence deepened, and the business became more sustainable.

Chloe's turning point wasn't about scale or strategy. It was about learning, seeing herself not just as a producer but as a leader willing to adapt.

Core Concepts: Entrepreneurial Learning as a Life Course Process

Entrepreneurship is often framed as a single choice, start or don't. But in reality, entrepreneurship is a learning journey across the life course. It intersects with personal identity, social roles, and transitions like career change, family formation, health events, or crisis recovery.

Filion (2023) described entrepreneurial learning as a convergence of competencies, vision, and relationships. He argued that entrepreneurs don't simply follow fixed pathways, they build new maps through reflective action.

Contemporary research supports this. Entrepreneurs are not merely decision makers; they are adaptive learners who make sense of ambiguous, rapidly changing environments (Souza and Wood 2022). Entrepreneurial learning often happens outside formal education, in moments of trial and error, identity conflict, feedback cycles, and informal mentorship.

Entrepreneurship is not a one-time act of starting up but a continuous learning journey shaped by personal identity, social context, and life transitions. Contemporary scholarship emphasizes that entrepreneurial learning unfolds less through formal education and more through iterative, experiential processes of trial, reflection, and adaptation (Fayolle 2020).

From Hustle to Reflection. Traditional portrayals of entrepreneurship endorse constant action and urgency. Yet research shows that sustained entrepreneurial success relies on reflective capacity, the ability to pause, interpret experiences, and integrate lessons into practice. Reflection transforms experience into insight and allows entrepreneurs to adapt beyond short-term fixes (Cope 2011).

Adaptive Entrepreneurship in Uncertain Environments. Entrepreneurs consistently face ambiguity, from shifting market dynamics to evolving personal responsibilities. Effective entrepreneurs do not eliminate uncertainty; they learn through it. Recent studies emphasize that adaptive leadership involves sensemaking, framing challenges as opportunities to learn rather than threats to stability (Uhl-Bien and Marion 2021).

Growth Mindset and Feedback. Foundational work on growth mindset continues to influence entrepreneurial research, but new contributions highlight the central role of feedback cultures within ventures. Leaders who model openness to feedback normalize learning behaviors in their teams, making the business itself a learning system (van der Heijden and Dijkhaizen 2021).

Failure as Fuel. Research increasingly reframes entrepreneurial failure not as an endpoint but as a key mechanism of growth. Post-failure reflection and experimentation are strongly correlated with resilience, opportunity recognition, and long-term success (Shepherd and Patzelt 2018). Building psychological safety in teams ensures that small failures can be openly discussed, reducing the cost of larger mistakes (Edmondson 2019).

The Life Course Perspective. Entrepreneurship is deeply entangled with biography. Life course theory highlights how identity, timing, and social roles shape entrepreneurial decision making. Recent scholarship shows that entrepreneurs encounter "developmental windows" where transitions, such as career changes, family responsibilities, or health events, open pathways for learning and reinvention (Singh and Gibbs 2021). This underscores that entrepreneurial identity is not static but evolves alongside the individual's life story.

Together, these concepts reframe the entrepreneur as a learner whose development is ongoing, relational, and responsive to context. Chloe's story illustrates this: Her venture grew not only through strategy but through her ability to reflect, adapt, and integrate personal transitions into her leadership practice.

The life course perspective deepens this view. According to recent contributions by Singh and Gibbs (2021), individuals encounter "developmental windows" throughout life, opportunities where experience, timing, and self-concept align to support growth. Entrepreneurial decisions are shaped by biographical context as much as by market analysis.

This approach helps us ask:

- What internal patterns shape our risk-taking?
- How do personal turning points influence our leadership style?
- What support systems enable or constrain our growth?

> *"Your capacity to learn is your greatest advantage. Stay curious. Stay open."*

Founder Spotlight

In Chloe's case, motherhood became a catalyst, not a constraint, for entrepreneurship. It redefined what productivity, time, and impact meant to her.

At first, Chloe measured success by independence. Doing it all meant she was in control. But over time, independence became unsustainable. Her leadership shifted in three ways:

- **Before:** Exhaustion, micromanagement, reactive decision making
- **After:** Delegation, reflection, and proactive leadership
- **Turning Point:** Weekly reflection practice and team trust

Her business grew not just in revenue but in resilience. She learned that independence is a starting point, but interdependence builds sustainability.

Entrepreneur Profile Snapshot

Founder: Chloe

Stage of Venture: Growth phase (early scaling)

What She's Building: Sustainable skincare rooted in local sourcing, self-care education, and mental health advocacy.

What Drives Her: Empowering others to slow down and reconnect with their own rhythms.

Learning Style: Visual, relational, and reflective.

Life Course Lens: Mid-career reinvention; parenting and purpose convergence.

Pivotal Learning Moment: Learning to delegate after burnout from solo production.

Quote

If I hadn't failed at trying to do it all alone, I wouldn't have found the courage to build a real team.

Table 3.1 *Entrepreneurial learning moments map*

Experience (turning point)	What I learned	How it changed me
1.		
2.		
3.		
Future Question	What do I need to learn next in order to grow sustainably?	

Visual Tool: Entrepreneurial Learning Moments Map

A reflection tool to surface learning patterns across the entrepreneurial journey (Table 3.1).

How to Use It:

- Choose three past experiences (a decision, a mistake, or a moment of courage).
- Write down what you learned and how it shifted your perspective, skills, or leadership.
- Add one future learning question that reflects the next stage of your journey.

This tool works for both individual reflection and team conversations. Here's Chloe's story translated into the Entrepreneurial Learning Moments Map. This way, you can see how to use the tool in practice (Table 3.2).

Table 3.2 Example: Chloe's learning moments

Experience (turning point)	What I learned	How it changed me
Leaving hospitality to start my skincare venture	I didn't need a perfect plan to begin, curiosity and resilience were enough to get started.	Gave me the courage to act on instinct and trust that I could learn along the way.
Balancing entrepreneurship with motherhood	Productivity isn't just about hours worked, it's about energy, focus, and presence.	Redefined my expectations of success and helped me design my business around sustainability, not exhaustion.
Burning out from doing all production myself	Trying to do everything alone limits growth and leads to exhaustion.	Taught me to delegate and trust others, which expanded capacity and made the business more resilient.
Future Question	How can I grow my venture without losing the values and purpose that make it meaningful?	

Practice in Action: Six Months with the Learning Map

Chloe revisited her Learning Moments Map strategically over six months. Here's what she found:

- **Month 1**: Admitted her exhaustion; set a goal to delegate packaging.
- **Month 2**: Noticed resistance from a part-time staff member; initiated a check-in conversation to clarify roles and expectations.
- **Month 3**: Noted improved energy; expanded delegation to client e-mails.
- **Month 4**: Faced new fear, "What if I lose control?" but realized trust built resilience.
- **Month 5**: Reflected on shifting from doing to leading; began documenting workflows to support future onboarding.
- **Month 6**: Added her future question: "How can I mentor my first full-time hire to lead with me?"

Lessons Learned:

- Delegation is scarier than overwork, but more powerful.
- Reflection creates clarity in chaos.
- Mentorship multiplies impact.

This tool invites you to trace three past turning points (e.g., decisions, mistakes, moments of courage) and one future question. It is designed as a simple quadrant visual or reflection prompt.

Talk About It with Your Team

Individual reflection is powerful, but entrepreneurial learning multiplies when teams reflect together. Use these prompts to spark team conversation:

- What patterns of learning show up in our decision making?
- How do we respond to mistakes, as opportunities or threats?
- What environments help us learn best?
- When do we avoid learning (e.g., repeating patterns, avoiding feedback)?
- What are we teaching others, intentionally or not, through how we lead?

Founder Spotlight: The Builder-Coach

Jordan runs a trades-based company. For years, he was the expert, answering every question, solving every problem. But as his crew grew, he realized knowledge wasn't spreading. Mistakes repeated, morale dipped, and he felt trapped.

When he introduced reflective "tailgate chats" at the end of each week, asking, "What worked, what didn't?" something shifted. Crew members began sharing insights. Trust grew. Jordan learned that leadership isn't about having all the answers, but about creating space where learning flows.

Founder Spotlight: The Maker-Founder

A café owner turned textile maker, Aisha found her biggest learning moments came not from success but from setbacks, when a product line flopped, or when balancing family care forced her to pause. Instead of hiding these struggles, she shared them with her team. The honesty created trust. Her venture thrived because people saw it as a place where growth was human, not mechanical.

Chapter Close and Transition

"In the rush to succeed, don't forget to stop and ask: What is this moment here to teach us?"

Entrepreneurs are not just builders of products; they are designers of living systems. Ventures succeed not by following a rigid blueprint, but by adapting, sensing, and evolving with their environment.

- **Feedback cycles** act like the nervous system of a venture. Insights from customers, employees, and partners flow back into decisions, keeping the system responsive.
- **Failure** functions as a reset mechanism. When something breaks, it reveals weaknesses in the system and creates an opportunity to reconfigure for greater strength.
- **Resilience** comes from diversity of thought, skills, and experience. Ventures with multiple perspectives can absorb shocks, adapt faster, and spot opportunities others miss.

A living system perspective reminds us that growth is less about linear expansion and more about adaptability, reflection, and renewal.

Across personas:

- **The Purpose-Driven Founder** learns to anchor growth in values.
- **The Builder-Coach** learns to pass knowledge through people.
- **The Emerging People Leader** learns to balance burnout with renewal.

Together, they illustrate this truth: We don't just grow businesses; we grow with them.

Entrepreneurs who embrace reflection and learning not only grow their ventures but grow into the leaders those ventures require. By seeing themselves as learners, founders create resilience, adaptability, and purpose that extend far beyond quarterly results.

But personal learning is only the beginning. The next step is designing businesses that learn with us. In Chapter 4, we will explore how to structure learning into the daily fabric of work, so that reflection becomes culture, not just crisis response. We'll look at huddles, roundtables, or talk sessions, mentorship practices, and feedback rituals that embed learning into the way a venture operates every day.

CHAPTER 4

Structuring Learning into Daily Work

Designing Growth from the Inside Out

Turning Point Opening Narrative: The Builder-Coach's Turning Point

Jordan leaned against the side of his truck at the end of another long week. The sun was dipping low, casting orange light across the job site. His crew, good men and women with solid skills, were packing up their gear. But Jordan couldn't shake the frustration gnawing at him.

Earlier that day, he'd corrected the same mistake he'd fixed three times before. It wasn't dangerous, but it cost time and wasted materials. Why aren't they learning? he thought. He'd shown them how. He'd explained it. Yet here he was again, patching over problems and carrying the weight of being the only one who truly knew how everything worked.

For years, Jordan prided himself on being hands-on. He could swing a hammer faster than anyone, solve problems in the moment, and keep projects moving. But as the business grew, so did the pressure. Every question, every crisis, came back to him. He was exhausted. And the dream of passing the business to his crew one day felt impossible if they couldn't carry leadership themselves.

That night, Jordan pulled out a notebook. Instead of writing down tasks, he listed questions: Why do mistakes repeat? What am I not seeing? What do they need from me to grow?

The next week, he tried something new. At the end of Friday, he gathered his crew around the tailgate. "What went well this week?" he asked. Silence. Then one worker mentioned a shortcut that saved time. Another admitted he'd almost botched a measurement but caught it. Soon, the stories flowed. It was messy, sometimes awkward. But it was real.

Over time, these "tailgate chats" became a rhythm. Mistakes surfaced earlier. Wins were celebrated. New hires learned faster. And Jordan realized something: His role wasn't just to get the work done. It was to build a system where learning happened every day.

Core Concepts: Learning as a Daily Practice

Entrepreneurship thrives when learning is not left to chance but built into the everyday rhythm of work. While Chapter 3 explored the entrepreneur as learner, Chapter 4 asks, How do ventures themselves become learning systems?

Research shows that when learning is embedded into routines, ventures are more adaptable, innovative, and resilient (Fayolle 2020; Marsick and Watkins 2018). Below, we explore five key practices.

Structuring Learning into Daily Work

Entrepreneurial learning is most powerful when it is iterative: act, reflect, adapt. Kolb's experiential learning cycle—which includes experience, reflection, conceptualization, experimentation—remains one of the most widely used frameworks for adult and organizational learning (Kolb 2015). For entrepreneurs, this means intentionally building reflection points into the workday rather than waiting for crises to force adaptation.

Practical routines like short "learning sprints" or weekly debriefs make learning visible and actionable. These rhythms normalize reflection, signaling that growth is part of the job, not a distraction from it.

Huddles/Roundtables and Mentorship

Learning is rarely a solo activity. It thrives in peer-to-peer contexts where people can test ideas, exchange feedback, and model practices. Rae (2006) found that entrepreneurial identity itself develops through relational learning, often in informal settings. More recent research confirms that mentorship enhances both confidence and resilience in entrepreneurial contexts (St-Jean and Tremblay 2020).

For small businesses, mentorship doesn't need to be formal. Pairing a new hire with a tenured crew member, running "peer sessions" where employees share weekly insights, or rotating responsibility for teaching a skill can all make learning collaborative and continuous.

Developmental Feedback

Too often, feedback in business settings is evaluative, focused on errors and outcomes. But developmental feedback emphasizes growth, helping individuals frame challenges as opportunities. London and Smither (2020) argue that developmental feedback builds stronger commitment and adaptability, especially in entrepreneurial environments where uncertainty is constant.

Creating a culture of feedback requires entrepreneurs to model openness. When entrepreneurs share what they are learning, mistakes included, it gives permission for others to do the same. This transforms feedback from criticism into collaboration (van der Heijden and Dijkhuizen 2021).

Learning as Culture, Not Program

Organizations often treat "training" as an add-on, a workshop here, a handbook there. But sustainable ventures treat learning as cultural infrastructure. Argyris and Schön (1996) described this as double-cycle learning: not only correcting mistakes but questioning underlying assumptions. When people see that reflection is woven into daily routines, whether in meetings, job sites, or customer interactions, they internalize learning as "the way we do things here."

This cultural lens is especially critical in small and medium-sized ventures, where adaptability can mean the difference between survival and stagnation (Marsick and Watkins 2018).

The Entrepreneur as Learning Designer

Finally, entrepreneurs must see themselves not just as builders of products or services but as designers of learning systems. Souza and Wood (2022) argue that entrepreneurial success increasingly depends on small business owners' ability to structure adaptive learning under conditions of uncertainty.

Jordan's story highlights this shift. He realized his role wasn't only to ensure the job was done but to shape the conditions in which his crew could develop, delegating stretch assignments, creating space for reflection, and embedding mentorship into workflow.

> *"Build the system that builds you, one step, one insight, one iteration at a time."*

Founder Spotlight: A Landscaping Business Scales Through Mentorship

When Rosa launched her landscaping business, she was the sole designer, salesperson, and foreperson. As demand grew, she hired a crew, but soon found herself answering the same questions daily, from job site procedures to client follow-up. Exhausted, she realized her business would stall if every problem still flowed back to her.

Instead of adding more rules, Rosa experimented with "learning sprints." Every Thursday afternoon, the team gathered for 30 minutes to reflect on one win and one challenge from the week. Out of these conversations came small process improvements, new client communication strategies, and even onboarding guides written by the crew themselves.

She also paired each new hire with a more experienced team member, not just for technical skills but for discussing resilience, client expectations, and confidence on the job. These informal mentorships reduced turnover and created a culture where "learning on the job" was valued as much as getting the job done.

Within two years, Rosa no longer fielded every question. Instead, her crew collaborated to solve problems, drawing on shared learning. Productivity improved, but so did morale. Employees described the business not just as a workplace but as a place to grow.

Rosa's story shows how small structural shifts, learning sprints, mentorship pairs, reflective practices, can transform a business into a learning-centered venture.

Visual Tool: The Learning System Map

The *Learning System Map* helps entrepreneurs make visible where and how learning happens in their ventures. By mapping current practices, entrepreneurs can identify strengths, gaps, and opportunities to embed learning into daily work (Table 4.1).

How to Use It:

1. List the channels where learning already occurs (peer, customer, self, mentorship, routines).
2. Capture current practices.
3. Add concrete examples.
4. Identify one improvement opportunity for each channel.

Practice in Action: Builder-Coach's Map

- **Peer Learning:** Jordan's crew often problem-solved in pairs. He formalized this by setting aside 15 minutes each Friday for "crew insights."

Table 4.1 Learning system map

Learning channel	Current practice	Example from builder-coach/ Rosa	Opportunities to improve
Peer-to-Peer Learning	Informal advice on job sites	Crew members share one win/one challenge each week	Formalize into short learning sessions
Customer Feedback	Occasional complaints or praise	Clients' recurring questions flagged during sprint meetings	Create simple log for recurring insights
Self-Reflection	Ad hoc journaling	Rosa's reflection before team sprints	Encourage each team member to share one insight
Mentorship	Unstructured "shadowing"	Pairing new hires with experienced crew	Rotate pairs to broaden exposure
Embedded Routines	Weekly staff meetings (task-focused)	Thursday "learning sprint" ritual	Expand to include client-facing stories

- **Customer Feedback:** He began recording recurring client questions in a shared notebook, which later became part of onboarding.
- **Mentorship:** Instead of leaving it to chance, he assigned new hires to work under his most reliable foreperson for the first month.
- **Routines:** Weekly meetings shifted from job scheduling only to include one reflection on "what we learned this week."

These small adjustments transformed his business from a set of tasks into a learning ecosystem.

Talk About It with Your Team

Use these prompts to make learning a shared responsibility:

- Where do we already learn well together?
- What learning gets lost in the rush to deliver?
- What feedback cycles feel safe, and which need improvement?
- What story from this week could teach us something for the future?
- How do we know when learning has become part of our culture?

Variations:

- **Small crews:** Keep it simple with verbal reflections.
- **Office-based teams:** Use Slack channels, Trello boards, or digital trackers.
- **Hybrid settings:** Record quick videos or voice notes to share lessons asynchronously.

Founder Spotlight: Six Months of Change

Jordan committed to weekly tailgate chats for six months. Here's what happened:

- **Month 1:** Crew hesitant; Jordan led by sharing his own mistake first.
- **Month 2:** Participation grew; one worker suggested a new measuring process that saved time.

- **Month 3:** Fewer repeated mistakes; new hire onboarded faster.
- **Month 4:** Crew started running chats themselves.
- **Month 5:** Jordan noticed less reliance on him for daily problem-solving.
- **Month 6:** Turnover risk dropped; foreperson emerged as a leader-in-training.

Lessons Learned:

- Modeling vulnerability builds trust.
- Simple rituals create cultural shifts.
- Empowering others lightens the founder's load.

Founder Spotlight: The Social Entrepreneur

Leila runs a community café. Early on, staff turnover was high and morale was uneven. Inspired by peer learning practices, she introduced short "reflection sessions" at the end of shifts: "What went well, what could be better?"

The practice-built trust quickly. Staff began suggesting menu ideas, community events, and even supply chain improvements. For Leila, the shift was clear: Learning wasn't just about coffee, it was about culture.

Chapter Close and Transition

"Scaling a business isn't just about what you grow, it's about what you grow through."

Entrepreneurs are not only builders of businesses; they are architects of living systems. A venture is dynamic, adaptive, and shaped by how learning flows through it.

- **Feedback cycles** are the nervous system: They carry signals that help the venture adapt.
- **Failure** is the reset mechanism: It surfaces weak points and demands reconfiguration.

- **Resilience** is adaptability: Ventures with diverse skills and perspectives weather shocks better than rigid systems.

When learning is structured into daily work, ventures evolve beyond dependency on the founder. They become ecosystems of shared growth. Across personas:

- **The Builder-Coach** learns to create space for his crew to grow.
- **The Purpose-Driven Founder** learns to anchor learning in values.
- **The Social Entrepreneur** learns that culture is built in small rituals.

The message is clear: If you want a venture that lasts, build it as a system where learning is visible, shared, and scalable.

Entrepreneurship is not only about personal learning; it's about creating ventures that learn with you. By structuring reflection, feedback, and mentorship into daily routines, entrepreneurs turn workplaces into learning communities. These practices don't just solve immediate problems, they build cultures of adaptability, resilience, and growth.

In the next chapter, we shift focus to the people inside these learning systems. How do we grow talent from within, ensuring that leadership, ownership, and confidence expand beyond the founder? Chapter 5 explores how mentorship, delegation, and informal learning shape the future of your business, often more than strategy ever could.

PART 2

People First, Always

Growing Talent from Within

Why Developing People Is the Smartest Growth Strategy

Turning Point Opening Narrative:
Martin's Turning Point

The smell of sawdust clung to the workshop floor as Martin stacked the final boards of the day. His team, a loyal group of tradespeople, had finished another contract on time and to spec. The quality was there; he had made sure of it. But Martin was exhausted.

Every measurement double-checked, every client question answered, every supplier issue negotiated, it all came through him. His crew could handle the technical work, but whenever something tricky came up, all eyes turned to Martin. He was proud to be the expert. But increasingly, he wondered: Am I holding us back?

One evening, as he closed the shop, Martin admitted the truth to himself: He was the bottleneck. He wanted to step back, maybe even prepare to hand the company to the next generation. But how could he if no one else was ready to lead?

The next day, instead of assigning tasks, Martin tried something different. He asked one of his forepersons to take the lead on a project. At first, the crew hesitated. They weren't used to decision making. But Martin stayed in the background, resisting the urge to jump in. Mistakes were made, but so were breakthroughs. Slowly, leadership began to spread.

Martin realized that building projects wasn't enough. If his business was going to thrive beyond him, he needed to build people.

Core Concepts: Growing People as a Strategy

Most entrepreneurs think growth means adding more: more clients, more staff, more output. But often the smartest growth strategy is to develop the people you already have.

1. **Apprenticeship and Stretch Roles**
   The oldest form of entrepreneurial learning is apprenticeship: watching, trying, failing, and improving under guidance. Today, apprenticeship can take many forms, shadowing, cross-training, or taking on stretch roles slightly beyond one's comfort zone.
   - A new crew member leading their first client walkthrough
   - A kitchen worker managing inventory for a week
   - A junior designer presenting in front of a client

   These moments grow confidence and capability. Research on the Igbo apprenticeship system in Nigeria shows that deep, experiential commitment produces resilient entrepreneurs across generations (Irene et al. 2024). The same principle applies everywhere: Real responsibility, supported by trust, accelerates growth. In Ontario, a small-town auto repair shop owner regularly takes on high school co-op students. One recent apprentice was invited to manage intake calls and build customer trust—an unusual responsibility for a teenager. But with coaching and real accountability, he thrived. Today, he's completing his Red Seal certification and plans to open his own garage in the same community.

2. **Delegation as Development**
   Delegation isn't just offloading tasks, it's intentional development. When framed well, delegation communicates trust and signals growth.
   - **Task delegation:** "Do this because I don't have time."
   - **Developmental delegation:** "Take this on because I think you're ready to grow."

   A study of small businesses found that employees stayed longer when they felt ownership of meaningful responsibilities (Ande-Global 2021). Growth happens when delegation is a pathway to leadership, not just efficiency.

3. **Informal Learning Every Day**

   Did you know that nearly 70 percent of workplace learning happens informally, through conversations, trial and error, and everyday reflection? Recent data (Association for Talent Development [ATD] 2024) confirm this trend, and ATD reports that in a third of organizations, informal learning makes up more than half of all development. The challenge is not whether learning happens, it's whether we capture it. Teams that build rituals like post-project debriefs or short end-of-shift reflections avoid repeating mistakes and build stronger cultures of trust.

   Simple questions like
   - "What went well today?"
   - "What could we try differently next time?"

   become powerful learning engines when repeated consistently.

4. **Talent as Culture Building**

   How you grow people becomes your culture. If learning is seen as punishment (fixing mistakes), employees will hide errors. But if learning is seen as growth (stretching, experimenting), people will lean in.

   Culture isn't built by slogans; it's built in how you respond under pressure. Do you punish risk, or do you frame it as part of learning?

5. **Formal Learning, Networks, and Associations**

   While this book emphasizes learning from experience, it's important to acknowledge the many excellent formal learning supports available:
   - **Colleges and universities** offer entrepreneurship courses, incubators, and applied research partnerships.
   - **Accelerators and innovation hubs** provide mentorship, funding opportunities, and structured growth programs.
   - **Associations, chambers of commerce, and trade groups** connect entrepreneurs to peers, resources, and advocacy.

   For example, many Canadian entrepreneurs tap into programs at MaRS Discovery District, Futurpreneur, StartUp Canada, or college-based incubators that combine mentoring with applied learning. These networks complement on-the-job reflection by broadening exposure, building peer support, and offering new perspectives.

Reflection prompt: What external learning opportunities could expand your growth right now, courses, associations, or mentorship networks?

"A business isn't just what you do, it's who you grow with."

Founder Spotlight: From Kitchen Staff to Leaders

When Priya opened her neighborhood restaurant, she expected long hours and constant hustle. She was right. For years, she worked from dawn until close, managing staff, cooking, ordering, customer service. It was unsustainable.

The real turning point came when she realized her best employees were leaving. They liked the work but saw no future beyond their current roles. Priya decided to change that.

She began giving stretch roles: asking a line cook to manage the weekly supplier call, inviting a server to handle a staff meeting, or encouraging a dishwasher to learn the grill. At first, mistakes happened. Orders were missed. Meetings were clumsy. But over time, her staff grew into leaders.

To reinforce growth, Priya started weekly "learning shifts." Each week, someone took on a different responsibility. She paired newer staff with veterans, turning everyday tasks into apprenticeships. She also sent two rising entrepreneurs to a local college's restaurant management certificate program, combining on-the-job growth with formal learning.

The results were transformative. Turnover dropped, customer reviews improved, and Priya finally had breathing room. Within three years, she promoted two managers from within. The restaurant thrived not because Priya did everything but because she grew leaders who could carry the vision forward.

Visual Tool: Internal Talent Growth Map

The *Internal Talent Growth Map* helps entrepreneurs identify how to grow people intentionally (Table 5.1).

Table 5.1 Internal talent growth map

Team member	Current role/ contribution	Untapped strengths	Development opportunity	Support/ mentor	Readiness for more responsibility
Sarah	Scheduling and invoicing	Tech-savvy, strong communicator	Training new hires on software	Office manager	High
Jamal	Crew member, 2 years' experience	Great with clients, reliable	Leading a small project	Foreperson mentor	Medium
Lina	Server, 1 year	Calm under pressure	Managing supplier calls	Priya	Emerging

How to Introduce with Your Team:

1. Share the tool openly, show that growth is intentional.
2. Involve team members in identifying their own strengths.
3. Pair development opportunities with support.
4. Revisit quarterly to track progress.

How to Use It:

1. List each team member.
2. Identify their current role and what they already contribute.
3. Capture untapped strengths you've noticed.
4. Define one development opportunity (a stretch role, skill, or responsibility).
5. Assign a mentor or support system.
6. Rate their readiness for more responsibility.

This simple map turns talent growth into a visible, intentional process.

Variations:

- **Solo founder with contractors:** Use the map to identify where external partners could take on more.
- **Small teams:** Keep it light, one development focus per person.
- **Larger teams:** Integrate into performance reviews or succession planning.

Practice in Action: Six Months of Growth

Priya committed to using the Talent Growth Map for six months.

- **Month 1:** Identified untapped strengths in three staff.
- **Month 2:** Introduced "learning shifts."
- **Month 3:** Promoted one team member to assistant manager.
- **Month 4:** Sent two staff to a certificate program.
- **Month 5:** Staff began running weekly check-ins themselves.
- **Month 6:** Customer satisfaction scores rose; turnover dropped.

Lessons Learned:

- Growth requires letting people stretch, even if messy at first.
- Pairing formal training with daily practice builds confidence faster.
- Developing leaders creates resilience and reduces founder burnout.

Talk About It with Your Team

Use these questions to spark meaningful team conversations that connect personal experience with how you build, lead, and grow together.

- Where do we already see people growing beyond their roles?
- What opportunities could we create for stretch roles this year?
- Who could be paired as mentor/mentee?
- What external supports (courses, associations) could we tap into?
- How do we celebrate growth, not just results?

Entrepreneur Profile Snapshot

Founder: Matthew
Business: Hillock Tree Care
Location: Ontario, Canada
Industry: Arboriculture and Urban Forestry
Years in Business: Since 2014

Matthew launched Hillock Tree Care out of a love for climbing and a strong desire to "work his own way." The business began with little more than a passion for the outdoors, a few essential tools, and an instinct that independence would push him to grow.

Turning Point

Hiring his foreman, and eventual partner, transformed Hillock from a solo venture into a collaborative, growth-oriented company. "People are what you give them," Matthew says. That moment reshaped how he led and how the business grew.

Learning and Leadership

Matthew's leadership style has evolved from managing tasks and critiquing quality, to something more foundational: cultivating growth. "I now see my job as creating an environment where people can learn and grow freely." "Whether it's giving new hires the chance to try bigger climbs or inviting experienced team members to train others, Hillock's culture of learning is hands-on and human."

Life Course Reflection

From a solo climber to a team-focused leader and father, Matthew's journey reveals how deeply identity and responsibility intertwine when building a venture from the ground up. Fatherhood changed the stakes. For Matthew, being present, at work and at home, is now central to how he defines leadership.

Core Learning

Micromanagement stunts learning. Trust builds it. Matthew's shift from being the expert to enabling others' expertise, through experimentation, reflection, and mentorship, changed everything. "I learned to lead by stepping back."

Work–Life Balance and Identity

Now a father, Matthew sees leadership through a different lens, one shaped by both greater empathy and higher expectations. "Getting home on time matters more than ever. But so does building something worth handing down."

Quote

> *You have nothing without strong relationships. The invisible ties that hold everyone together matter more than your bottom line. Your relationships will rescue you over and over. Long-term growth depends on goodwill.*

Chapter Close and Transition

"When you grow people, you grow possibility."

Delegation, apprenticeship, and informal learning are not luxuries, they are the hidden engine of small business growth. By investing in the people you already have, you create a stronger culture, a deeper bench of leadership, and a business that doesn't rely solely on you.

Ventures are living systems. Their sustainability doesn't come from the founder alone, but from the adaptive capacity of their people.

- **Feedback cycles** ensure lessons don't get lost.
- **Delegation** becomes the system's way of spreading intelligence.
- **Mentorship** builds continuity across generations.
- **Formal networks** inject new ideas and perspectives.

Across personas:

- **The Builder-Coach** learns to pass the torch.
- **The Emerging People Leader** learns to navigate burnout by developing others.
- **The Purpose-Driven Founder** learns that values scale best when people embody them.

The message is clear: Growing talent is not a side project; it is the core of building ventures that last.

In Chapter 6, we'll build on this foundation by exploring culture as your true competitive advantage. Because how you grow people isn't just a strategy, it becomes the way your business is experienced every single day.

Culture Is Your Competitive Advantage

How Shared Values and Psychological Safety Shape Thriving Ventures

Turning Point Opening Narrative: How You Work Is What You Build

The sound of chainsaws hummed in the background as Matt tightened his harness, preparing to scale another towering oak. His tree care company had grown steadily over the years, bigger contracts, more crews, more gear to manage. For a while, he measured success by efficiency: how quickly jobs were completed, how many trees they could clear in a day, and how fast they moved from one site to the next.

But one autumn afternoon, he noticed something that changed his perspective.

A new hire froze halfway up a trunk. The climb wasn't especially difficult, but the rookie was clearly rattled. Instead of mocking him or shouting orders, the senior climber on the ground called up calmly: "Take a breath. Pause and assess. You're safe. We've got you." The new hire steadied himself, made his cut, and returned to the ground a little shaken, but smiling.

Later, Matt overheard the crew talking. They weren't swapping stories about efficiency or deadlines. They were talking about trust. About how the team always had each other's backs. About how mistakes were shared, not punished.

That was the moment Matt realized: It wasn't speed or scale that set his company apart. It was culture.

From that day, he began to invest not only in equipment and contracts but in the invisible system of values, trust, and behaviors that shaped how his team worked together.

What Matt discovered that day is something many entrepreneurs realize only after a few growing pains: The invisible forces that shape your team's behavior, your culture, are far more powerful than any business strategy on paper.

Core Concepts: Culture as the Hidden Advantage

Culture isn't the posters on your office wall or the mission statement on your website. It's how people actually behave when the pressure is on, when the boss isn't watching, and when things go wrong.

In small and growing ventures, culture is more than a "nice to have." It's the operating system of the business.

Culture as Operating System

Every decision—from how you greet a client to how you handle a mistake—is filtered through culture. Do people speak up when they see a risk? Do they cut corners when deadlines loom? Do they share credit or hoard it?

When entrepreneurs design culture with intention, they shape how the business responds in the everyday moments that matter most.

One of the clearest signs of an intentional culture is whether people feel safe enough to speak up when it matters. That's where psychological safety comes in.

Psychological Safety

At the core of a strong culture is psychological safety, the confidence that you can speak up without fear of embarrassment or punishment. In big corporations, this idea often gets framed in HR policy. But for entrepreneurs, it shows up in much simpler ways:

- A team member admitting they miscalculated an estimate
- A new hire asking a "basic" question without being mocked
- A foreperson suggesting a change to a long-standing routine

When people feel safe to share concerns, mistakes, or ideas, you catch problems earlier and surface innovations faster.

Safety is just one part of the equation. It's also about what your team believes in, and whether their daily actions reflect those beliefs.

Shared Values in Practice

Values aren't what you say. They're what you do consistently, especially under pressure.

It's easy to say "we value safety" until a client pushes for faster delivery. It's easy to say "we respect people" until deadlines are missed. Culture is revealed in these moments. Do you stick with your stated values, or do you compromise them?

Entrepreneurs who align actions with values build credibility, both with their teams and their customers. And when those values are consistent and visible, culture becomes more than a feel-good concept. It becomes your edge in the marketplace.

Culture as Strategic Advantage

When culture is strong, it attracts talent, deepens customer loyalty, and drives sustainable performance. People want to work where they feel respected. Clients want to hire teams who radiate trust and professionalism.

For Matt's tree care company, culture wasn't a side benefit. It became the very reason clients chose him over competitors. But culture isn't something you can afford to ignore or leave undefined. Whether you've built it deliberately or not, it's already shaping your outcomes.

You Already Have a Culture

Every business has a culture, whether you design it or not. The question is: Is yours intentional?

Culture forms from daily behaviors, unspoken rules, and repeated choices. By pausing to reflect, you can see where your culture is helping you, and where it's quietly holding you back.

That's why regular reflection matters. The following tool helps you step back and examine what kind of culture is forming in your business, and how you might strengthen it.

> *"Culture isn't a perk. It's your signal, your strategy, your future."*

Visual Tool: The Culture Reflection Checklist

The *Culture Reflection Checklist* helps entrepreneurs step back and assess the culture they are building. Use it quarterly, or whenever your team is going through transition or growth (Table 6.1).

This checklist isn't about perfection. It's about noticing patterns, making small adjustments, and keeping your cultural compass pointed in the right direction.

To see how these ideas come to life, let's look at Trina's HVAC business, where fast growth exposed cracks, and a culture reset brought the team back on track.

Table 6.1 The culture reflection checklist

Reflection question	Why it matters	Action step
What behaviors are rewarded, formally or informally?	People repeat what gets recognized. If only speed is rewarded, safety or quality may erode.	Identify one behavior you want to highlight this month (e.g., collaboration, initiative).
When pressure hits, which values hold up, and which fade?	Values are tested under stress. If they disappear when deadlines loom, they aren't real.	Name one value you refuse to compromise on, even under pressure.
Who feels safe to speak up, and who doesn't?	Psychological safety is uneven. Some voices may dominate while others stay silent.	Ask one quieter team member for input in your next meeting.
Are learning, feedback, and failure welcomed or avoided?	Avoided failure becomes repeated failure. Openness builds innovation and resilience.	Try a short "what we learned" reflection at the end of a project.
What rituals or routines reflect our shared identity?	Rituals make culture visible. Without them, values remain abstract.	Start or reinforce one simple ritual (e.g., daily huddle, weekly gratitude).

Mini-Case: Solving the Growth Trap—Trina's HVAC Business

Trina launched her HVAC company with a single truck, one apprentice, and a reputation for being the kind of person who didn't cut corners. Business grew fast, too fast. Within a year, she had six techs, a packed schedule, and cracks starting to show.

One install was signed off too quickly. A final check was skipped. A client complained. Not because of danger but because the attention to detail she'd built her name on had slipped.

That weekend, Trina pulled the team in and asked two simple questions:

1. "What's the standard we want to be known for?"
2. "What's making it harder to keep it?"

The answers surprised her: Newer staff weren't sure what was expected. No one wanted to look weak by asking. Her culture hadn't scaled with the team.

So, she created a one-page "Field Code" together:

Check twice. Speak up early. Own your work. Have each other's backs.

She paired it with a clear principle: "If in doubt, do the thing that earns trust, not speed."

Within months, the work improved. Clients noticed. Trina didn't just fix an internal communication issue; she strengthened her brand through her culture.

Culture becomes especially powerful when it helps people make decisions with the future in mind, not just reacting in the moment but responding in ways that reinforce long-term trust and adaptability.

Decision Making and Future Orientation

Culture becomes your competitive advantage when it helps your team make good decisions under pressure, not just when things go according to plan. When entrepreneurs like Trina make decisions with the future in mind, it helps the team adapt to change, respond quickly to new information, and stay grounded even as the business scales. That's not fluff—that's strategy.

Matt's story offers another lens into this transformation, where small rituals around safety evolved into a culture that defined his business at every level. Tools help us reflect, but stories show us what's possible. To see how culture can transform a business in practice, let's return to Matt's world of tree care, where safety rituals turned into a powerful culture that shaped not only performance but also trust, loyalty, and growth.

Founder Spotlight: Tree Care and the Power of Safety Culture

When Matt first introduced "pause and assess" rituals before every climb, some of his crew rolled their eyes. They wanted to get moving, get the job done. But over time, the ritual stuck. It wasn't about slowing down, it was about protecting each other.

He began scheduling monthly crew debriefs, nothing fancy, just regular check-ins at team gatherings to talk through what was going well, where mistakes were creeping in, and what could make things run smoother. They shared near misses, small wins, and lessons learned. At first, team members hesitated. Who wanted to admit a mistake? But as Matt modeled openness, talking about his own close calls, the team followed suit.

Mistakes declined. Junior staff began speaking up about hazards before they escalated. New hires quickly absorbed the culture because it was practiced daily, not just written in a handbook. Clients noticed, too: Word spread that Matt's company was not only reliable but deeply professional.

For Matt, culture became his true competitive advantage. Safety was more than compliance, it was a visible expression of respect, professionalism, and team cohesion. Whether you're just starting out or expanding your team, pausing for a conversation about culture can strengthen alignment and surface what matters most.

Talk About It with Your Team

Use these questions to spark a values-based conversation:

- What's one value we want to see more of in our daily work?
- What unspoken rules shape how we operate?
- What kind of culture do we want new team members to feel on day one?
- How do we show respect for each other, especially under pressure?

These aren't just reflective prompts, they're culture-shaping moments. Every conversation, every response to pressure, every team ritual either reinforces or erodes the culture you're building.

Chapter Close and Transition

"Culture is the invisible contract your business makes with every person who enters it."

Every business has a culture. The question is whether yours is intentional, consistent, and aligned with your values. When you make culture your competitive advantage, you create an environment where people thrive, clients trust you, and growth becomes sustainable.

But culture is not static. It's tested in moments of uncertainty and change. In Chapter 7, we'll explore how culture holds steady, or shifts, when entrepreneurs face burnout, identity transitions, and reinvention. We'll look at what it means to navigate change with a human lens, leading not only with strategy but with empathy and resilience.

CHAPTER 7

Navigating Change with a Human Lens

Leading Through Uncertainty, Identity Shifts, and Renewal

Turning Point Opening Narrative: Entrepreneurship at the Edge of Uncertainty

When Amanda signed the papers to sell her recruitment agency, she expected relief. The business had been her life's work for over a decade. She'd built it from a one-woman operation into a respected regional firm, guiding clients through countless hiring challenges. Financially, the sale was a success. She had stability, security, and the freedom to rest.

But the next morning, Amanda woke to silence. No buzzing inbox. No urgent client calls. No team to check in on. For years, her identity had been intertwined with her business. Now, despite the payout, she felt unmoored.

Weeks turned into months. Friends congratulated her, but Amanda wrestled with a different reality: *Who am I without my business?*

She didn't launch another venture right away. Instead, she slowed down. She tried her hand at pottery, knitting, woodworking, simple, tactile acts that grounded her. Then, what began as a hobby grew into something more. Eventually, Amanda opened a small creative studio where she blended craft with coaching, helping others find meaning through making.

Her story is a reminder that change isn't always a quick pivot. Sometimes it's a process of realignment, of rediscovering yourself, rebuilding from the inside out, and learning to lead from a place of wholeness rather than sheer productivity.

Core Concepts: Leading Change from the Inside Out

Entrepreneurs often think of change in external terms, new markets, shifting industries, evolving customer needs. But the hardest changes are often internal. They test identity, values, energy, and relationships as much as strategy. Navigating change with a human lens means recognizing these undercurrents, not just the surface-level shifts.

Leading Through Uncertainty

Change brings uncertainty, and uncertainty triggers anxiety, for founders and for teams. It's not just, "What will happen to the business?" but also, "What will happen to me?"

Entrepreneurs who navigate uncertainty well don't pretend to have all the answers. Instead, they normalize openness:

- Naming what is known and unknown.
- Creating space for questions, even when there aren't clear answers.
- Modeling calm curiosity instead of forced certainty.

This doesn't mean sugarcoating hard truths. It means leading with honesty and presence. When entrepreneurs acknowledge uncertainty without panic, they create stability for others to find their footing.

Burnout and Renewal

Many entrepreneurs ignore burnout until it becomes impossible to hide. The signs are familiar: fatigue, irritability, loss of creativity, and disengagement. Burnout is not just a personal issue; it ripples into decision making, team morale, and customer relationships.

Renewal requires intentional design. For some, it means stepping back for a season. For others, it's building recovery into daily rhythms, exercise, journaling, or community rituals. Some founders use sabbaticals, creative outlets, or quiet mornings as a way to recharge.

The point isn't the method. It's the recognition that you can't pour from an empty cup. Businesses led by depleted entrepreneurs eventually show the strain. Renewal is not indulgence; it's fuel for sustainable leadership.

Identity Transitions

Entrepreneurship is often an identity as much as a role. Selling a company, stepping back from day-to-day operations, or shifting industries can trigger identity loss. Entrepreneurs may ask: *If I'm not the founder, who am I?*

These transitions, while painful, are also opportunities for growth. They invite reflection:

- What roles have I outgrown?
- What parts of my identity endure, regardless of the business?
- How do I want to show up differently in the next chapter?

Identity transitions are not about erasing the past but integrating it into a new story. Amanda's move from recruiter to maker illustrates this: She didn't abandon her skills; she reframed them in a new context.

> *"You're not expected to have all the answers. But you are expected to grow with the questions."*

These moments of identity change aren't theoretical, they shape real lives, careers, and legacies. Amanda, once a recruitment entrepreneur, offers a powerful case of what it means to lead through personal transformation.

Entrepreneur Profile Snapshot: Recruitment Agency—Beyond Hiring

This entrepreneur led a recruitment agency focused on aligning people with purpose-driven careers. With a background in operations, she transformed a personal layoff experience into an opportunity to create a values-based business model that emphasized transparency, fairness, and long-term fit. Her journey reflected the interplay of identity, business ownership, and systemic change.

Business Overview

A recruitment agency specializing in executive and mid-career placements with a focus on values alignment, client integrity, and candidate advocacy.

Entrepreneur's Journey

The founder's journey began after experiencing a layoff, leading her to reassess what meaningful work looks like. Combining industry insight with a people-first approach, she built a company designed to support both clients and candidates with equal integrity.

Turning Points

Her decision to start the business was catalyzed by personal adversity. As her agency grew, she expanded from local placements to broader national-level work, and began advising clients on inclusive hiring practices.

Business Values

Transparency, equity, integrity, and purpose-driven growth. She prioritized systemic change in hiring through advocacy and education.

Key Learning Moments

Learning to say no to clients who don't align with the company's values; investing in her team's learning; balancing advocacy with profitability.

Future Vision

Expand leadership development services; deepen impact on inclusive hiring systems; scale through mentorship-based models rather than traditional franchising.

Life Course Reflection

This entrepreneur transformed a deeply personal experience of job loss into a people-first business that challenged the status quo of traditional hiring.

> **Quote**
>
> *I used to think the right job was about the title or the salary. After being laid off, I realized the right work is about fit, values, energy, and purpose. I didn't want to just place people in roles. I wanted to help them find where they truly belong, and help employers recognize the power of getting that right.*

Culture Across the Life Course: A Living Thread Through the Stages of Business

Culture isn't something you build once and then leave behind. It's a living thread that moves through each life and business stage, evolving as your leadership, identity, and priorities shift. This life course perspective challenges the idea that culture is a "start-up phase" issue. In fact, it becomes more important as the business matures.

In Early-Stage Ventures:

Founders often focus on survival. Culture forms through instinct and proximity: how decisions are made, how trust is built, and how people feel when they show up to work. These early practices create the emotional blueprint.

In Growth Phases:

Culture becomes stretched. New hires, remote work, systems, all add complexity. If culture is not intentionally revisited, early values may erode. Founders who evolve their culture in this phase ensure it remains aligned with their purpose and team needs.

In Transition or Exit Phases:

As entrepreneurs hand off operations, culture needs to be transferrable. This requires documentation, storytelling, and shared rituals. Culture becomes a legacy, something you leave behind not just in systems but in people.

By understanding culture as a life course element, one that adapts to your age, energy, goals, and lived experience, you can lead with greater clarity. Whether you're in your 30s building momentum, or your 60s rethinking your role, culture is your human fingerprint on the organization.

Culture Grows with You: Life Course Reflections

Culture is not just a system you enforce; it's a living reflection of your values and your way of responding to uncertainty. And because you grow, evolve, and face new realities across your career, so too must your culture.

A growing body of research, including work by Louis Jacques Filion (2023) and others in entrepreneurial education and developmental psychology, emphasizes that leadership is not static. Entrepreneurs change. We are shaped by our life course: the personal, social, and professional transitions we experience across time.

Culture, then, is not one moment in your business plan, it's a moving mirror. It reflects the values you held when you started and adapts as you move through seasons of growth, disruption, and renewal.

Whether you're navigating your first hire or considering succession planning, your beliefs, identity, and focus shift. Founders who are aware of their own life course can design more flexible, responsive cultures that make room for both stability and change.

Three Life Course Moments That Shape Entrepreneurial Culture

1. **Identity-Building at Start-Up**
   Early in the business, founders often imprint their personal values directly into team dynamics. Long hours, shared sacrifice, and a bias for action shape culture organically, but this also risks creating fragility if not later made explicit.

2. **Growing and Letting Go**
   As teams grow and operations expand; culture must be carried by more than the founder. This is when reflection matters most. Your past choices, what you tolerated, how you communicated, what you avoided, may come back to challenge your intentions.

3. **Reorientation and Legacy**
   Mid-career and later-stage entrepreneurs often re-engage with culture not from a place of urgency, but purpose. They ask bigger questions: *What kind of place have I built? Who do I want to become next?*

Pause and Reflect:

- How has your leadership changed since you started?
- Are there habits or beliefs you've outgrown that your culture hasn't?
- What kind of environment do you want to build *now*, and why?
- What's one "lesson from life" you've applied (consciously or not) in shaping your business?

Visual Tool: Your Entrepreneurial Life Course Map

1. **Look Back**

   List two key transitions (personal or professional) that have shaped your leadership. What values emerged from these moments? (Table 7.1).

2. **Look at the Present**

   What's one decision you've made recently that reflects your current cultural values?

   What does it say about what matters to you right now?

3. **Look Forward**

   What kind of culture will your business need in three to five years?

   What habits or systems will you need to build today to support that future?

Change as a Learning Invitation

The most resilient entrepreneurs see change not only as disruption but as invitation. Even difficult transitions carry insights, about priorities, limits, values, or blind spots.

Table 7.1 Your entrepreneurial life course map

Transition	What changed?	Value that emerged
Example: Becoming a parent	Time constraints, clarity of focus	Empathy, boundaries
Example: Losing a cofounder	Rebuilding from crisis	Trust, transparency

When entrepreneurs frame change as a question ("What can we learn here?") rather than just a problem ("How do we fix this?"), they process disruption into resilience. This mindset doesn't minimize the pain of change; it transforms it into fuel for growth.

Founder Spotlight: From Recruiter to Maker

Amanda's story is one of unraveling and reweaving. For years, she thrived on building a recruitment agency. But when she exited, she faced the disorienting question of who she was without it.

At first, she felt lost. She tried volunteering, consulting, even considered starting another agency. Nothing clicked. Then, almost accidentally, she began experimenting with craft. Pottery classes led to hours at the wheel. Knitting turned into conversations with local makers. Slowly, a new identity emerged, not just as a business builder but as a creator.

Her creative studio began small, with workshops blending craft and coaching. People came not only to learn a skill but to reconnect with themselves. Amanda's leadership shifted, too. She no longer defined success solely by productivity or revenue. Instead, she measured it by connection, meaning, and wholeness.

Her journey reminds us: Change doesn't always mean reinvention. Sometimes it means realignment, finding your way back to purpose in a new form.

The Entrepreneur's Reflection Cycle

The *Entrepreneur's Reflection Cycle* is designed for small business owners in flux, those facing endings, transitions, or reinventions. It provides simple prompts to guide decision making when the ground feels unsteady (Table 7.2).

How to Use It:

- Use during transitions: new hires, scaling, exits, burnouts, or reinventions.
- Reflect individually or with your leadership team.
- Return to it quarterly to check alignment.

Table 7.2 The entrepreneur's reflection cycle

Reflection prompt	Why it matters	Example
What is ending?	Acknowledging endings prevents carrying old baggage forward.	"My role as the sole decision maker is ending as I hand more responsibility to my team."
What is emerging?	Spotting early signals helps you seize opportunities.	"A new line of services is gaining traction."
What is calling for attention?	Emotions and relationships matter as much as strategy.	"Team morale is low; we need to pause and reconnect."
What values must remain constant?	Values are anchors during disruption.	"Respect and inclusion remain nonnegotiable, even if our structure shifts."

Talk About It with Your Team

Try these prompts in a team retrospective or leadership retreat:

- How has change impacted us emotionally, not just operationally?
- What do we need to let go of, and what do we want to carry forward?
- Where are we resisting change, and where are we ready to grow?
- What values do we want to hold steady, no matter what shifts?

Culture Pulse Across the Business Life Course

Use the following tool to reflect on how your leadership stage, and life stage, may be influencing the culture of your business today (Table 7.3).

Reflection Prompts: Culture, Change, and Identity

These prompts can help entrepreneurs and small business owners integrate the emotional and cultural dimensions of change into daily leadership.

- What beliefs or habits shaped our early culture, and do they still serve us?
- Where has the business outgrown my current way of leading?

Table 7.3 Culture pulse across the business life course

Stage of business	Culture strengths	Culture risks	Key questions to ask
Early Stage (Start-Up)	Energy, closeness, shared hustle	Burnout, unclear values	What kind of workplace am I building by default?
Growth Phase	Momentum, expanded talent	Drift from original values	Are we scaling culture intentionally, not just headcount?
Transition/ Succession	Wisdom, reflection, mentorship	Identity loss, culture dilution	What legacy am I leaving behind? How do I preserve it?

- How does my current life stage influence what I value and how I show up?
- What signals (positive or negative) are we hearing from our team about culture right now?
- If someone joined us today, what would they feel about how we work and relate?

Chapter Close and Transition

Change doesn't ask you to have a plan; it asks you to pay attention—to your people, your purpose, and yourself. Because the culture you shape through those moments becomes your lasting imprint.

Change is inevitable. But whether it fractures or strengthens your venture depends on how you navigate it. Entrepreneurs who bring a human lens, attending to identity, emotions, values, and renewal, create resilience not just in themselves but in their teams.

Moments of change often generate the most valuable insights, if we know how to capture them. In Chapter 8, we'll explore how to make learning visible and scalable inside your venture, using rituals, tools, and team practices that transform experience into culture and reflection into performance.

PART 3

Embedding Learning into Growth

Making Learning Visible and Scalable

From Individual Insight to Shared Growth

Turning Point Opening Narrative: From Individual Insight to Shared Growth

In a growing professional legal services firm, the founder began noticing something troubling. Staff were learning incredible lessons, on client calls, through project mistakes, and during tough feedback, but those lessons weren't being shared. Each person was learning in isolation. Knowledge stayed siloed, and mistakes repeated themselves.

So she tried something simple. Every Tuesday, the team gathered for a 30-minute ritual they called "Tuesday Reflections." Each week, one person told a short story about something they had learned recently.

At first, the stories were small: a client objection that was handled well and a project that ran over time. But soon, the practice took on a life of its own. Team members began sharing deeper insights about communication, resilience, and leadership. New hires were onboarded faster, because they were hearing real stories instead of just reading manuals. The ritual became a culture builder, a coaching ground, and a way to turn experience into growth.

Meanwhile, across town in a solo legal consultancy, a former law firm partner had left behind the trappings of success to create something different, a purpose-driven, people-first legal practice grounded in reflection. For her, learning wasn't scaled across a team but deepened through pause and discernment. She began journaling after each client engagement and relied on peer learning through small professional circles, where stories were exchanged not for speed but for substance.

While the two founders operated differently, one scaling team rituals, the other anchoring reflective solo practice, they shared a common truth: Learning must be intentional. Whether echoed in a shared room or held quietly in a journal, it only creates change when it's seen, named, and used.

Core Concepts

Learning as a Team Asset

When learning is shared, it multiplies. A lesson discovered by one person can prevent mistakes, inspire innovation, and raise confidence across the entire team. Treating learning as a collective asset turns growth from an individual pursuit into a team advantage.

Storytelling and Rituals

Stories turn moments into meaning. A weekly reflection, a short debrief, or even a shared "what worked/what didn't" can carry more weight than a formal report. Rituals like "Tuesday Reflections" give structure, signaling that learning isn't optional or occasional, it's part of how the team operates.

Making Learning Visible

Left unspoken, learning fades quickly. Visible practices, like shared journals, peer check-ins, coaching conversations, or even a whiteboard where insights are posted, capture what might otherwise be lost. Visibility builds accountability and reminds people that growth is ongoing.

Team-Based Learning Systems

Learning isn't a side project. For sustainable ventures, it becomes a rhythm embedded into operations. That might mean starting meetings with a "learning check-in," closing projects with a reflective debrief, or pairing team members to exchange skills. Teams that systematize learning outperform those that treat it as an afterthought.

Recent studies on micro-enterprise learning cultures (Filion 2023) suggest that owner-managers often develop informal but powerful knowledge routines, often rooted in life experience, past trades work, or sports disciplines, that later become the foundation for scaling. These systems reflect the entrepreneur's own learning biography, evolving through trial, peer feedback, and client results. By making them visible, founders create future-ready team norms.

From Knowledge Hoarding to Knowledge Flow

Some workplaces reward individuals for holding onto information. But people-first ventures flip the script: Knowledge is shared freely. When entrepreneurs model openness, they replace scarcity with abundance. What one person learns can help the whole team succeed.

Making learning visible doesn't have to mean writing in a notebook or pinning notes to a whiteboard. Today's teams capture learning in Slack channels, shared digital boards like Trello or Notion, or even short Loom videos. What matters isn't the tool; it's that the insight doesn't stay hidden in one person's head.

> *"Growth with intention beats speed without direction."*

But how do we move from intention to implementation? Let's explore the practical tools teams are already using to turn shared learning into action.

Digital/Tech-Enabled Learning Practices

1. **Shared Digital Boards (e.g., Miro, MURAL, Trello, Asana)**
   Instead of a physical whiteboard, teams can keep a live "learning board" where insights, reflections, or process tweaks are captured.

- ○ *Example:* A Trello card titled "What We Learned This Week" where team members add quick notes

2. **Team Chat Integrations (e.g., Slack, Microsoft Teams)**
Dedicated "#learning" or "#wins-and-lessons" channels let people drop short reflections in real time.
    - ○ *Example:* A quick post after a client call: "We found this question helped uncover hidden needs."

3. **Micro-Videos or Voice Notes**
Short Loom videos, screen captures, or even voice memos allow people to share what they've learned quickly, in a way that feels more natural than writing.
    - ○ *Example:* A two-minute screen recording showing how to fix a recurring software glitch

4. **Collaborative Knowledge Hubs (e.g., Notion, Confluence, Google Docs)**
A living "playbook" where lessons learned, best practices, and client insights are logged for easy access by the whole team.
    - ○ *Example:* New hires can browse "lessons from the field" in a Notion database.

5. **Pulse Surveys and Quick Feedback Tools (e.g., Mentimeter, Kahoot!, Google Forms)**
These let teams gather insights and reflections during or after projects, capturing patterns across the group, not just individuals.
    - ○ *Example:* A quick Friday pulse asking: "What did you learn this week?" with results shared on Monday

6. **Social/Peer Learning Platforms**
Younger employees are accustomed to sharing knowledge socially (like Instagram stories or TikTok). Teams can leverage this instinct in a work-friendly way:
    - ○ *Example:* Create an internal "micro-story" series where each week a different person shares a short post, meme, or clip capturing a lesson.

In Canada, hubs like MaRS Discovery District have embraced this shift by offering their programs entirely online, making resources, mentorship, and peer learning available to entrepreneurs across the country. From Yukon to Nova Scotia, founders can now access learning networks and coaching digitally, reflecting the way global work is changing—hybrid, accessible, and always connected (MaRS 2023).

Technology helps, but it is mindset and consistency that anchor learning in a team's DNA, as this founder's story illustrates.

Founder Spotlight: Coaching as Culture

One founder of a mid-sized coaching firm wanted to build a culture where reflection wasn't left to chance. She introduced short-form coaching questions into team check-ins. Each person was invited to name:

1. A current tension they were navigating,
2. A lesson they had learned recently, and
3. A small experiment they were trying next.

At first, people hesitated, sharing tensions felt risky. But over time, the practice became normal. Blame decreased, curiosity increased, and uncertainty was no longer something to hide. Performance improved, but so did resilience.

The founder's insight was simple: Reflection doesn't require long sessions or elaborate programs. Small, consistent practices, built into existing rhythms, can normalize learning across the team.

While coaching firms may have structured check-ins, other sectors apply the same principles in everyday routines. Let's meet one such entrepreneur. This profile acts as a real-world example of how learning becomes visible and embedded into a growing client-based service venture. It reinforces the coaching and culture-building themes from the previous section.

Entrepreneur Profile Snapshot: Fitness and Personal Training—Strength from Within

Business Overview

A boutique fitness and performance training business offering personalized coaching, specialized programs, and small group sessions for clients seeking strength, transformation, and long-term wellness. The business operates from a well-equipped private studio with a growing client base and strong local reputation. Adults aged 25 to 60 seeking personalized fitness programs, including professionals, athletes, and individuals recovering from injuries or navigating health changes.

Entrepreneur's Vision and Mission

To transform the lives of clients by providing expert, evidence-based training in a supportive, personalized environment. The mission centers on building both physical capacity and personal confidence.

Unique Approach and Philosophy

Focusing on whole-person wellness, emphasizing individualized coaching, accountability, and education. Programs are designed with long-term sustainability and measurable outcomes in mind, avoiding fitness fads.

Growth Journey and Lessons

The business has grown organically through referrals and results-driven outcomes. Key lessons include the importance of client relationships, ongoing learning, and adapting services to changing needs and lifestyles.

Key Challenges

Balancing capacity with demand, navigating the shift to virtual/hybrid training during the pandemic, and maintaining business momentum while prioritizing personal wellness.

Opportunities Ahead

Expanding into online coaching, launching wellness retreats or specialty programs, and partnering with health professionals to offer more holistic services.

Strategic Insight

This venture reflects the importance of consistency, trust, and long-term relationship building in service-based industries. The founder leverages their own athletic background and community roots to foster a loyal client base.

Life Course Reflection

Before opening the fitness studio, this entrepreneur spent years in athletics and personal training, constantly surrounded by transformation stories, both physical and emotional. But starting the business brought a deeper level of growth. They confronted insecurities, built systems, and learned to lead not just clients but a team. Becoming a business owner was all about shifting from individual performance to collective purpose. It taught how to be a coach in every sense, inside and outside the gym.

Quote

I used to train people's bodies. Now I help shape careers and confidence too.

Profiles like our Fitness Entrepreneur remind us that scalable learning is built one moment at a time, if we take time to notice. Now it's your turn to reflect.

Visual Tool: The Learning Practices Tracker

The *Learning Practices Tracker* helps individuals and teams visualize where learning is happening, and where it could be made more intentional (Table 8.1).

How to Use It:

- As a team, list where learning already happens.
- Identify one improvement in each area.
- Revisit quarterly to keep learning visible and scalable.

Talk About It with Your Team

Use these questions to spark meaningful team conversations that connect personal experience with how you build, lead, and grow together.

Table 8.1 Learning practices tracker

Practice area	Current examples	Opportunities to improve
Weekly Rituals	Tuesday reflections, project debriefs	Add short peer teaching segments
Coaching Conversations	One-on-one check-ins	Normalize micro-coaching in team huddles
Feedback Cycles	Client surveys, post-project reviews	Capture more "real-time" customer feedback
Self-Assessment and Journaling	Individual notebooks	Share one insight in team meetings
Peer Teaching and Mentorship	Informal shadowing	Rotate mentors to spread knowledge

- Where are we learning, but not yet capturing that learning?
- What routines could make learning more visible in our work?
- How do we celebrate reflection, not just results?
- What knowledge could we share that would make someone else's work easier?

Mini-Tool: "Learning Touchpoints Map"

- Identify three recurring activities your team already does (e.g., Friday clean-up, shift swaps, sales check-ins).
- For each one, answer:
  1. What small learning usually happens here?
  2. How could we make it just a little more visible?

Example: During post-session huddles at the gym, staff already debrief on client progress. By capturing one insight each week in a shared doc, our fitness entrepreneur's team built a simple reference tool for junior coaches.

Chapter Close and Transition

"Learning is the strategy. If we make it visible, we make it scalable."

Every venture produces learning. The question is whether it stays hidden with individuals or becomes a shared asset for the team. By making learning visible through rituals, storytelling, and tools, you create resilience that grows with your business.

In Chapter 9, we'll look ahead to the future of work, where generational shifts, hybrid teams, and inclusive leadership are redefining how ventures must adapt. Making learning scalable is step one; designing for the future ensures that learning stays relevant in the long run.

CHAPTER 9

Designing for the Future of Work

Inclusive, Flexible, and Built to Evolve

Turning Point Opening Narrative: Inclusive, Flexible, and Built to Evolve

The conference room buzzed with questions about artificial intelligence, automation, and the "future of jobs." Most of the audience were young professionals, tablets open, phones ready. For many, the language on stage, full of acronyms, technical jargon, and abstract forecasts, felt impenetrable. They wanted to understand, but the speakers seemed to be talking past them.

Sitting near the back, Sinead Bovell (https://www.sineadbovell.com/aboutsinead) noticed the gap. She saw a generation hungry to engage with the technologies shaping their lives, but locked out by inaccessible language and elitist conversations. These weren't "tech people," yet technology would define their futures.

That night, she scribbled in her notebook: *What if we made these conversations accessible? What if we created a space where anyone, not just coders or executives, could understand and shape the future of work?*

Soon after, she launched WAYE (Weekly Advice for Young Entrepreneurs), a platform built on one simple belief: The future of work should be inclusive. She translated complex concepts into plain language, blending workshops, digital talks, and social media storytelling. Instead of intimidating technical lectures, she hosted interactive sessions where participants could ask anything, from "What is AI bias?" to "How do I navigate a hybrid workplace?"

Sinead's approach resonated. Younger entrepreneurs, especially Millennials and Gen Z, were craving more than strategy, they wanted meaning, autonomy, and fluency in the digital shifts reshaping their work (Deloitte 2025). Through WAYE, she created not just a resource but a community—one that valued curiosity over credentials, inclusivity over hierarchy, and participation over passive consumption.

Her vision wasn't to build the next "big tech" start-up. It was to democratize knowledge. To make sure future workplaces were designed not just by experts in boardrooms but by the diverse voices of those who would live and lead in them. Today, WAYE reaches hundreds of thousands globally, yet it remains rooted in a distinctly Canadian sensibility: pragmatic, inclusive, and people-first (Bovell, n.d.).

Sinead's journey captures what this chapter is about: designing ventures for the future of work that are flexible, inclusive, and globally relevant, ventures where learning is accessible, culture is intentional, and leadership is built with tomorrow in mind.

Core Concepts: What the Future of Work Demands

The future of work is not just about automation, algorithms, or hybrid schedules. It's about how entrepreneurs design ventures where people can thrive across generations, contexts, and rapid change.

1. **Generational Shifts**

   Millennials and Gen Z make up an increasing share of the workforce. They bring expectations that differ from previous generations: autonomy, inclusion, flexibility, and impact. They don't want to be "managed" in the traditional sense. They want leaders who coach, workplaces that align with their values, and systems that allow for flexibility (Deloitte 2025).

   Research also shows that Gen Z in particular is wary of burnout. Many are actively avoiding traditional management roles, preferring collaboration and shared leadership models over rigid hierarchies (Business Insider 2025). For entrepreneurs, this is a wake-up call: attracting and retaining next-generation talent means creating environments where well-being and growth are integrated into daily work.

2. **Remote and Hybrid Realities**

The pandemic accelerated what was already coming: distributed work as a norm. Even small businesses now juggle hybrid or flexible arrangements. The challenge is not just logistical; it's cultural. How do you build trust and cohesion when people aren't always in the same room?

Teams that succeed in hybrid environments invest in intentional rituals, from weekly check-ins to digital "learning channels" in Slack or Teams. Tools like Trello, Notion, or Loom make collaboration visible. Canadian hubs like MaRS Discovery District have fully digitized their entrepreneurial support programs, showing how learning can be made accessible coast to coast, in real time (MaRS 2023).

The principle is simple: If your systems aren't designed for hybrid, they aren't designed for the future.

3. **Inclusive Leadership**

Inclusive leadership isn't an HR initiative; it's a business imperative. Studies show that inclusive leadership directly improves adaptability and innovation, particularly for Gen Z employees (Katsaros 2024). Canadian research confirms that younger employees expect diversity, equity, and inclusion (DEI) to be prioritized, 72 percent say they would decline a role if an organization lacked real DEI commitments.

Inclusive leaders:
◦ Actively invite diverse perspectives.
◦ Ensure every voice can be heard safely.
◦ Recognize that identity, background, and lived experience shape how people engage at work.

In practice, this might mean changing hiring processes, rethinking communication norms, or simply ensuring team meetings rotate who speaks first. Small shifts create workplaces where people don't just "fit in"—they *belong*.

4. **Future-Proofing Through Learning**

The best way to prepare for uncertainty is to build learning into your culture. Ventures that treat reflection and adaptation as core practices can pivot faster, seize opportunities earlier, and weather disruption with less friction.

This is where tools like learning trackers, digital playbooks, and peer storytelling become critical. They allow teams to capture lessons in real time, instead of reinventing solutions later. The future belongs not to the ventures that avoid mistakes but to those that learn from them visibly and quickly.

Entrepreneur Profile Snapshot: Connection, Culture, and the Courage to Pivot

Industry: HR Tech, Events and Experience Design, Workplace Culture

Location: Washington, DC, the United States, and Remote-first

Entrepreneur: Sharon—Connector, Founder, Systems Thinker, Culture Architect

Business Focus: Offsite and experience planning for culture-forward workplaces

Clients: HR teams, People and Culture leaders, Fortune 500 companies, scaling start-ups

Offerings

- Curated employee experiences (virtual, in-person, hybrid)
- Offsite planning and execution
- Culture and connection strategy for remote and distributed teams

Signature Approach

Translate company values into joyful, authentic employee experiences that foster belonging, connection, and retention.

Turning Point

The business began as a mobile app for finding happy hours and social spots. It quickly gained traction in Washington, DC, but the onset of COVID-19 made its entire business model unsustainable overnight. Instead of folding, Sharon pivoted. She leveraged her relationships with venues and creators to build immersive, meaningful virtual experiences, from culinary kits to cocktail classes, that helped companies stay connected during lockdown. This bold reinvention didn't just save the business; it brought increases in revenue and established the business as an early innovator in the virtual event space.

Core Learning

"Connection is the heart of culture, and culture is how you win."

Sharon's greatest insight is that workplace culture isn't about ping pong tables or perks. It's about experiences that reflect a company's values. Her business is a strategic partner to HR and leadership teams, helping them invest in moments that create trust, joy, and psychological safety.

Designing for the Future of Work

Sharon led a successful post-pandemic pivot that centered purpose and adaptability. Her model supports hybrid and distributed teams, reinforcing inclusion through intentional experiences. Her leadership embodies resilience, emotional intelligence, and people-first design. She also challenges the traditional start-up narrative, proving that re-defining success on your own terms is a radical, strategic act.

Life Course Reflection

"As a daughter of immigrants, I was taught to seek stability. But I craved freedom, to speak truthfully, build boldly, and not shrink myself to fit a system that wasn't made for me."

Sharon's story reflects the lived tension of many entrepreneurs: honoring legacy while designing a new path. Her transition from founder to founding team member at a new venture shows how entrepreneurs can evolve roles without abandoning identity, scaling impact while protecting energy.

Quote

There's no company without the humans who show up every day to make it real.

Resilience Reflection: Redefining Growth Without Burning Out

When Sharon founded Happied, she imagined a joyful tech platform that helped people connect through shared experiences, happy hours, team socials, community gatherings. When the pandemic forced her to shut down the very experiences her company relied on, she didn't give up. Instead, she reimagined the business, as a virtual experience and offsite planning business that would go on to generate more revenue and serve distributed teams across the U.S.

But success wasn't linear. Sharon learned that pivoting early isn't failure, it's wisdom. That "sticking it out" isn't always leadership, sometimes, letting go is. After leading through hypergrowth, she chose to scale herself back, preserving the business while transitioning to a founding team member role at a new mission-driven venture.

Her story reframes resilience as more than endurance. It's the ability to adapt, reflect, and reclaim energy without losing your values.

Reflection Prompts:

- What would it mean for you to redefine success on your terms?
- Where in your entrepreneurial journey are you holding on when it might be time to reimagine or release?

Legacy and Innovation

Designing for the future doesn't mean discarding the past. Many ventures thrive by integrating legacy, values, traditions, or long-standing relationships, with new practices. Think of a family business that keeps its deep sense of trust and reputation while adopting e-commerce or digital marketing. Or a trades-based company that holds onto craftsmanship while experimenting with new green technologies.

> *"The future of work isn't arriving, it's being shaped by entrepreneurs like you."*

Why the Future of Work Needs Entrepreneurs

While much of the conversation around the future of work focuses on employees, trends, or technology, we rarely ask the most urgent question: What kind of entrepreneurs does the future demand?

Entrepreneurs are not just responding to change; they are shaping it. The decisions they make about how they hire, build, relate, and grow don't just define their businesses. They influence the social contract of work itself. In an era of uncertainty and transformation, entrepreneurial leadership is becoming a civic force.

Entrepreneurs as Architects of Meaning

Research from McKinsey (2024) and the ILO (International Labour Organization, 2023) indicates that as traditional corporate paths become less stable, entrepreneurship is emerging as a key site of purpose, identity, and agency, especially for younger generations and underrepresented groups. Whether out of necessity or aspiration, people are choosing to build their own workplaces when existing ones don't reflect their values.

This shift means entrepreneurs are no longer just economic actors. They are meaning-makers. They build environments where work reflects personal and community values, autonomy, inclusion, equity, creativity, wellness.

Research consistently shows that when people don't find meaning in their work, they disengage, quietly or loudly. We're living through a time where people are questioning not just how they work but why they work. When purpose fades, so does performance, and often, participation. That's why so many modern ventures are fueled by a desire to reconnect work with values, identity, and social contribution.

From Job Creators to Culture Builders

The Organisation for Economic Co-operation and Development (OECD 2023) notes that small- and medium-sized enterprises (SMEs) account for more than 90 percent of businesses and over 60 percent of employment across OECD countries. Yet what matters most isn't just how many jobs they create, but what kind of jobs.

This is where entrepreneurial culture becomes vital. Are you building a hustle machine or a healthy ecosystem? Are you perpetuating burnout culture or designing for flexibility and growth? Every decision, from your first hire to your pricing model, signals how your business contributes to society.

When you build a venture, you're not just hiring. You're prototyping the future of work. One decision at a time.

Mini-Case: Nehal—Building a People-First Tech Venture in a Post-Corporate World

After nearly a decade climbing the corporate ladder in a multinational software company, Nehal reached a breaking point. He had the title, the pay, and the perks, but not the purpose. His team was burned out, diversity was performative, and innovation felt like a buzzword, not a practice. In his words, "I had everything I thought I wanted, but I felt like I was building something I wouldn't want my kids to work in."

So Nehal left. At first, he wasn't sure what came next. But after freelancing with nonprofits and coaching emerging tech entrepreneurs, a new idea began to take root: a digital product studio that prioritized ethical tech, inclusive leadership, and talent from nontraditional backgrounds.

Today, his company builds purpose-driven platforms for clients in health, education, and sustainability. But just as importantly, it models the future of work in its own operations:

- **Remote-first and flexible-by-design**: His team spans three time zones and sets their own working hours, built around life and caregiving responsibilities.
- **Distributed decision making**: Project leads rotate, and every team member participates in quarterly planning and retrospectives.
- **Mentorship from day one**: Nehal pairs new hires with peer coaches, not just to learn the tools but to feel heard, seen, and supported.

- **Hiring for potential, not pedigree:** The team includes bootcamp grads, career shifters, and community college alumni—all with lived experiences driving innovation.

For Nehal, entrepreneurship became a way to rewrite the rules, not just for how work gets done but for who gets to shape it. "I didn't set out to start a company," he says. "I set out to build a workplace I could believe in."

Reflection Prompt: What Are You Prototyping Through Your Venture?

Entrepreneurship is more than delivering a product or service; it's a powerful form of cultural and organizational design.

Consider:

- What values are embedded in how you hire, schedule, communicate, or make decisions?
- How does your business model reflect the kind of work culture you want to grow?
- Where are your systems inclusive, and where might they still reflect outdated assumptions?
- If your venture became the norm, what would the future of work look like?

What's one small change you could make this quarter to align your venture more closely with the future you want to see? What workplace norms are you ready to retire? What workplace practices are you proud to pass on?

Entrepreneurial Growth as Social Infrastructure

Future-of-work research increasingly recognizes that we need new social infrastructure to support a society in transition (Bregman 2025; Susskind 2024). Entrepreneurial ecosystems, hubs, co-ops, collectives, learning networks, can provide that infrastructure.

Canada's own Innovation Superclusters and community entrepreneurship accelerators (e.g., MaRS, Communitech, Futurpreneur, Black Innovation Programs) are beginning to take on this role, but their reach depends on founders who choose to grow in inclusive, relational, and values-driven ways.

Entrepreneurs, then, are not just building businesses. They are building bridges, between sectors, between generations, and between what work was and what it could be.

Entrepreneur Profile Snapshot: Insurance Sector— Passing the Torch: A Multigenerational Approach to Trust

Industry Overview

The entrepreneur operates in the financial services and insurance sector, an industry known for regulation, complexity, and deep reliance on trust. The firm provides life, health, and disability insurance alongside financial planning and investment services.

Business Foundation

Founded on the belief that insurance and financial services should be more relational than transactional, the business positioned itself as a partner in life transitions. Instead of simply selling products, the entrepreneur built an advisory practice centered on financial literacy, integrity, and care.

Market Positioning

The firm emphasizes values-based planning. Education is prioritized over sales pressure. Most growth comes through referrals and reputation, reflecting a client experience that is personal, transparent, and trustworthy.

Growth and Adaptation

Over the years, the firm has evolved with both client needs and workforce expectations. They invested in digital tools to meet clients online, while continuing community workshops that built intergenerational trust. Recognizing that the future of the business depends on developing younger advisers, the founder created mentorship pathways to ensure continuity and innovation. This transition honors legacy while preparing for the expectations of Millennials and Gen Z, who demand flexibility, autonomy, and meaningful work.

This story highlights the balance between legacy and innovation. The founder grew the business on long-standing values of trust and service but is now reimagining the workplace for a new generation of advisers. Through mentorship, hybrid engagement, and inclusive practices, the firm is actively designing for the future of work, ensuring the venture remains relevant in a rapidly evolving, people-first economy.

Life Course Reflection

The founder's journey has been shaped by intergenerational dynamics, both at home and in the business. Taking inspiration from past mentors while creating space for the next generation, they embody the principle that the future of work is not about replacing tradition but about integrating it with new practices.

Quote

The most valuable asset we pass on isn't a policy or portfolio, it's the trust and wisdom that prepare the next generation to lead.

Founder Spotlight: Inclusive Futures in Practice

When Sinead Bovell launched WAYE, she didn't just create a platform for young entrepreneurs, she modeled a new kind of leadership. By making technology accessible and inclusive, she showed how ventures can anticipate generational shifts, embrace hybrid realities, and build cultures of learning.

Her story is one among many Canadian examples: ventures that integrate values with adaptability, tradition with innovation, and inclusion with growth. Whether you're leading a family business in transition or launching a digital-first start-up, the principles remain the same: The future of work must be designed with people at the center.

Visual Tool: The Future-Fit Venture Canvas

The *Future-Fit Venture Canvas* helps entrepreneurs assess how their business aligns with evolving workforce expectations and leadership practices (Table 9.1).

How to Use It:

- Use in annual planning or strategy retreats.
- Score each section 1 to 5 and identify priority gaps.
- Revisit yearly to ensure alignment with evolving expectations.

Talk About It with Your Team

Use these questions to inspire thoughtful team conversations that bridge personal experience with shared leadership and growth.

- What do our next-generation team members want to grow into?
- What legacy is worth protecting, and what needs to evolve?
- How are we designing a workplace that future employees would choose?
- If our venture were built from scratch today, what would we design differently?

Table 9.1 Future-Fit Venture Canvas

Canvas section	Reflection questions	Example in practice
Talent Engagement	Do team members feel autonomy, meaning, and flexibility?	Offer hybrid hours, allow project choice.
Systems Inclusion	Are hiring, communication, and decision systems inclusive?	Diverse hiring panels, anonymous feedback.
Learning Infrastructure	Do we support growth through coaching, peer learning, experimentation?	Monthly peer sessions, skill-swaps.
Technology and Workflow Design	Do our tools reflect how Gen Z works?	Slack threads, Loom recaps, Notion hubs.
Legacy Integration	What traditions are worth keeping? Which need reimagining?	Preserve client relationship rituals, modernize pricing models.

Real-World Story: A New Generation Embraces the Future of Work

For today's entrepreneurs, "work" is no longer just about income or status; it's about alignment, agency, and adaptability. Madison's story below illustrates how a young business owner is designing not just a service-based venture but a work–life philosophy rooted in well-being, self-expression, and sustainable client relationships.

Mini-Case: Madison—A New Generation of Entrepreneurial Energy

Madison didn't wait for someone to hand her the blueprint. From the moment she stepped into her high school co-op salon placement, she knew she wasn't just learning a trade, she was discovering a language of creativity, care, and connection. That early exposure led her to a top hair institute in Toronto, where she graduated with honors in cut and color.

Six years later, her business opened its doors. But for Madison, the business was never just about hair. It was about wellness, expression, and individualized care, where clients, regardless of age, gender, or background, felt truly seen.

"Good hair reflects your story," she says. "And I get to help people tell that story, on their terms."

What sets Madison apart isn't just her technical skill. It's the way she's woven future-of-work principles into her small business:

- **Health and Autonomy**: Madison built her schedule around her energy, wellness, and creative rhythms. Her ability to choose her own hours directly supports mental well-being and client satisfaction.
- **Sustainability and Values**: Certified organic styling and color products are standard at her studio, not a luxury. Her clients value the health-first approach just as much as the results.
- **Personalization and Relationship**: Clients don't walk into a busy salon, they enter a private, one-on-one setting. Many have

followed her from early apprenticeships to her current business.
Her work feels relational, not transactional.

- **Marketing with Purpose**: Madison's "mom-ager" helped shape
her early promotional strategy. Today, she leverages local engagement and Instagram storytelling to attract new clients who align
with her brand, without spending on ads she doesn't believe in.

Turning Point

Madison's entrepreneurial journey began in high school through a co-op
at a local salon. Her passion deepened as she attended a prestigious hair
institute in Toronto, graduating with an honors degree as a coveted Dual-
ist, specializing in both hair styling and coloring. Launching "The Cut &
Colour Lounge" was her moment of transformation—from stylist to visionary business owner. Making it through her first year in business, especially during the uncertainties of start-up life, solidified her commitment.

Perhaps most telling is the pride Madison takes in "making it through
her first years" a milestone that many businesses never reach. Her satisfaction stems not from vanity metrics but from proving that it's possible to
lead a values-driven business while still thriving.

Continued Education

Continued education is a cornerstone to staying relevant. Madison has
added to her service offerings by becoming Great Lengths™ Certified
giving her the opportunity to provide hair extension services to her client. In addition, she actively engages with social media content and
follows thought leaders and educators in her field to stay informed and
inspired.

Future-of-Work Signals

Entrepreneurs like Madison offer a window into what the future of work
already looks like for those building it from the ground up. As you think
about your own work, whether solo or with a team, how many of these
"future-of-work signals" are you designing for?

Table 9.2 Future-of-work signals

Future-of-work signal	What it looks like in practice	Where you are today
Purpose-Driven Autonomy	You make decisions based on your personal values, wellness, and long-term goals, not just market trends.	☐ Early ☐ Evolving ☐ Embedded
Flexible Structures	You've designed your workday, location, or service model around how you work best, and allow clients to benefit.	☐ Early ☐ Evolving ☐ Embedded
Client-Connected Brand	Your clients feel like part of your community, and marketing is a form of authentic storytelling.	☐ Early ☐ Evolving ☐ Embedded
Sustainability (Personal and Planet)	Your services, tools, or products consider long-term environmental or emotional impacts, yours and others'.	☐ Early ☐ Evolving ☐ Embedded
Learning-Minded and Adaptive	You seek out new skills, test ideas, and adjust with new information instead of clinging to rigid models.	☐ Early ☐ Evolving ☐ Embedded
Meaningful Milestones	You celebrate growth through milestones that matter to you, not just money or scale.	☐ Early ☐ Evolving ☐ Embedded

Use this quick diagnostic to assess how aligned your entrepreneurial practice is with the evolving future of work (Table 9.2).

Madison's story is one of many emerging voices reshaping our understanding of work. These entrepreneurs aren't just coping with new paradigms; they're creating them. Their ventures are simultaneously expressions of identity, experiments in autonomy, and models of the future-ready workplace. They show us that entrepreneurship is not just economic activity; it's culture building at work.

Life Course Reflection

Madison's story reveals how early exposure, vocational education, and familial support can lay the foundation for entrepreneurial identity. Her career isn't accidental, it was shaped over time by meaningful formative experiences. She represents the value of pathways that blend hands-on experience with formal training, especially in creative or service-driven sectors.

Reflection Prompts

- How does your current or future work reflect your values?
- In what ways are you designing for flexibility, identity, or sustainability?
- What does thriving look like for you, and how might your definition evolve over time?

Chapter Close and Transition

"The future of work isn't a trend. It's a leadership responsibility."

The world of work is shifting quickly, but the future isn't something that happens to you, it's something you design. Entrepreneurs who embrace inclusion, hybrid realities, and continuous learning create ventures that are not only relevant but resilient.

As we move into the next chapter, we'll step back from the details and look at the bigger picture: your venture as a living system. What you choose to design today, your culture, your practices, your values, shapes not only the future of your business but the leader you are becoming.

CHAPTER 10

Your Learning Legacy

Networks, Mentorship, and Community

A leader is not the one who climbs the mountain fastest, it's the one who brings others with them.

Why Chapter 10 Is Different—A Note to the Reader

Chapter 10 intentionally departs from the structure used throughout this book. While earlier chapters focus on specific tools, frameworks, and founder spotlights, this chapter acts as a capstone—zooming out to explore the broader ecosystems, relationships, and intergenerational influences that shape entrepreneurial learning. Legacy is not a single moment or technique; it is an accumulation of experiences, stories, and shared knowledge.

For that reason, this chapter blends narrative, research, examples, and reflection to offer a more fluid, holistic exploration. It is designed to help readers integrate everything they've learned across the book and see themselves as part of a larger learning community. This structural shift is purposeful: It signals that entrepreneurial learning ultimately widens, connects, and continues beyond any single chapter or tool.

From Builders to Bridge Makers

The path of an entrepreneur often begins with a focus on starting, surviving, or scaling. But over time, many discover their impact reaches beyond the borders of their own venture. Whether it's mentoring a younger entrepreneur, supporting a community initiative, or advising others in the industry, business builders often become bridge makers, connecting others, sharing what they've learned, and influencing systems.

This is where learning turns outward. This is where leadership becomes legacy.

Not every business leader sets out to leave a mark. But many of the most meaningful contributions entrepreneurs make happen quietly, in peer conversations, apprenticeship guidance, or the wisdom passed down over coffee chats. These acts aren't flashy. But they shape industries, strengthen communities, and ripple into futures we can't yet see.

Entrepreneurial Ecosystems: Why They Matter

We often think of entrepreneurship as an individual pursuit. In reality, no one builds alone. Every venture is supported by a web of influences: mentors, collaborators, suppliers, local institutions, digital communities. When you recognize this, your role as a learner expands, you become both a contributor and a connector.

Entrepreneurial ecosystems include:

- **Local networks** like small business groups, chambers, or trade alliances
- **Peer mentorships** between founders at different stages
- **Sector-specific alliances**, conferences, or professional learning groups
- **Intergenerational networks** where legacy meets fresh perspective

Strong ecosystems aren't built on competition alone, they're built on shared learning and mutual investment. And that learning often happens in informal, unexpected moments: sharing a hiring process that worked, talking through burnout, and inviting someone to shadow a tough client meeting.

Case in Point: Marvin's Trade Network

When Marvin sold his HVAC (heating, ventilation, and air-conditioning) company after 30 years, he didn't picture himself "working" again.

But something pulled at him. He remembered how hard it had been starting out, how few people shared real numbers, trusted referrals, or admitted when they were struggling.

So he started small: inviting two apprentices from different companies to coffee. Then mentoring three early-stage trades entrepreneurs. Before long, he was facilitating a local peer group of HVAC, electrical, and roofing contractors. They talked operations, growth, and pricing—but also burnout, family succession, and mental health.

Marvin wasn't chasing scale anymore. He was building learning infrastructure, and that infrastructure was creating better businesses, stronger relationships, and a more resilient trade community.

> *"I used to think legacy was about selling the business for a big number. Now I know it's about leaving the industry better than you found it."*

The Learning Ecosystem

To help you reflect on your extended impact, consider the Learning Ecosystem below.

Your Learning Ecosystem:

1. **Who supports your growth?**
   Mentors, colleagues, peer networks, service providers, community hubs

2. **Who learns from you?**
   Team members, apprentices, mentees, clients, social media audiences

3. **What spaces enable your learning?**
   Formal learning, informal chats, partnerships, reflection, trial and error

4. **Where do you contribute back?**
   Advisory boards, mentorship, resource sharing, community support

Try drawing this out. Use arrows. Make it messy. The point isn't perfection; it's awareness. You're not just a leader of your venture. You're a part of a living system of learning.

Entrepreneur Profile Snapshot: Building a Business, Building Others

Founders: Maya and Felix, Collaborative Landscapes

Maya and Felix started their landscaping company with two things: a shovel and a dream. What they grew was far greater than a business, it's a model for apprenticeship, inclusion, and neighborhood renewal.

With a background in sustainable design and community development, Maya and Felix built their company around values. They hired newcomers to Canada and those restarting careers. They introduced monthly learning days for their crew, covering everything from native plant species to financial literacy. They started a shared mentorship program with a nearby trades business.

As Maya and Felix's venture matured, they realized their real passion wasn't just in building landscapes, it was in building people. They now facilitate a cross-business mentorship circle, coaching other founders in embedding training into their operations, and collaborate with city planners to design green spaces that reflect local identities.

Maya and Felix's impact? It's visible in gardens, of course. But it's also alive in the confidence of their apprentices, the trust of their clients, and the leadership emerging in the businesses they supported.

Reflection Prompts:

- Where in your business journey have you shared what you've learned? Where could you?
- What would it mean to intentionally contribute to the learning of others?

Learning as Legacy: What Will You Pass On?

Legacy isn't just about retirement. It's about what you're already leaving behind, how you communicate values, grow people, and shape systems.

Ask yourself:

- What do people say about what it's like to work with me?
- What learning practices would I want to pass on to others?
- How can I create space for those coming up behind me?

And perhaps most importantly: What kind of ecosystem leader am I becoming?

"You're not just building a business. You're creating a legacy of learning, one conversation, one connection, one act of generosity at a time."

Surrounded by intergenerational entrepreneurial influence, community support, and genuine excitement, enjoy this enterprising young entrepreneur's start-up story.

Entrepreneur Profile Snapshot: Lemonade, Legacy, and Little Hands

Entrepreneur: BBC (age 4)
Business: BBC's Driveway Lemonade
Industry: Beverages (pop-up style)
Location: End of the driveway, Suburban Street, Ontario, Canada
Supervisors: Mom (entrepreneur and educator), Dad (first responder), and Grandparents (retired business owners)

Business Overview

Armed with a folding table, a handmade crayon sign, and a pitcher of ice-cold lemonade, 4-year-old BBC launched his first business at the end of his family's driveway on a sunny July morning. What started as a simple stand quickly became a neighborhood moment of connection.

But this wasn't just any lemonade stand. It opened on Fridays, garbage collection day, because BBC had noticed how hard the maintenance workers worked in the summer heat. His goal? To offer them something cold and kind. It was his way of saying thank you.

Each cup of lemonade came with something extra: a small sheet of stickers. Whether you were a waste collector, a cyclist, or a passing police officer, everyone got a little smile-to-go. For BBC, it was important to offer something "one of a kind."

What Sparked the Idea?

However, this idea came about, BBC's idea seemed to come from a burst of excitement on a warm morning. One moment he was playing with crayons, and the next he was asking if he could "make something and sell it too." While he may not have understood the word *entrepreneur*, his family encouraged his curiosity. They helped him plan the stand, mix the lemonade, and practice how to greet customers. In a household where creativity and initiative are celebrated, BBC's playful question sparked a small venture, and a big memory. So the family turned it into a learning adventure: how to greet customers, count change, pour safely, and say thank you.

Lessons in Real Time

- **Confidence**: BBC stood proudly behind his stand, welcoming each customer with a big smile.
- **Math in Motion**: He practiced basic counting, coins, cups, and people.
- **Feedback Cycle**: He asked customers, "Do you like it?" and took their smiles seriously.
- **Resilience**: When he spilled his first cup, he wiped it up and said, "Oops! Try again."

Mini-Reflection from Mom and Dad

"Watching him learn how to connect with people, take pride in his setup, and get excited when someone stopped to buy a cup, it reminded me why I started my own business in the first place. It wasn't about the money. It was about seeing something I made bring someone joy."

Why This Story Matters

BBC's story may seem small, but it reveals something powerful: Entrepreneurship isn't just about scaling; it's about spirit. When a child is encouraged to explore, to create, and to take initiative, especially in a family or community that values entrepreneurial thinking, we plant the seeds for confidence, ownership, and possibility.

Reflection Prompts: From Crayons to Capital

- What if we treated entrepreneurial curiosity like a muscle?
- What would it look like to nurture that spirit in the young people around us?
- What if your next brainstorm started with a 4-year-old's question: "Can I try?"

Research Update: Learning, Legacy, and the Health Care Connection

Recent studies continue to highlight the enduring influence of informal learning, intergenerational knowledge transfer, and community-based leadership, particularly within mission-driven sectors like health care. For example:

- **Singh and Gibbs (2021)** emphasize how entrepreneurs experience identity shifts across the life course, particularly in community-embedded ventures. This perspective reinforces that legacy is not something "left behind," but something actively shaped through relationships and daily actions.
- **Heijden and Dijkhuizen (2021)** explore the importance of feedback culture within entrepreneurial teams, suggesting that creating space for open dialogue and shared meaning-making is foundational to legacy creation.
- **Marsick and Watkins (2018)** and **ATD (2024)** further support the idea that incidental learning, the unplanned but

transformational lessons that occur through peer conversation, mentorship, and reflective action, plays a major role in what entrepreneurs pass on.

These findings affirm that legacy isn't a future event. It's the accumulation of lived learning, something that resonates powerfully in people-centered sectors like health care.

Entrepreneur Profile Snapshot: Leading Through Care and Community

Founder: Amira
Business: Wellness Cooperative

Health care rooted in community, healing, and holistic learning.

Amira began her career as a nurse practitioner in a public health clinic, where she quickly recognized the deep gaps in continuity of care, especially for underserved populations. After years of witnessing burnout, fragmented systems, and patient frustration, she imagined a different model: a community-based wellness cooperative offering wraparound support, shared decision making, and culturally responsive care.

Her entrepreneurial path was not just about filling a gap but reimagining what healing could look like. Amira built a team of allied professionals, nurses, mental health counselors, community health workers, who engaged in weekly collaborative learning sessions. Her cooperative prioritized mentorship, from onboarding peer support workers to creating community education series.

Today, this business serves both rural and urban communities. Amira's legacy is visible in patient stories, in the leadership roles her team members have taken on, and in the systems-level policy discussions she now contributes to. She continues to mentor early-career health entrepreneurs and serves on advisory boards focused on community-based care models.

> **Quote**
>
> *Legacy isn't just about what you build, it's about how many others learn to build because of you.*

As we reflect on what we leave behind, our values, practices, stories, and ways of working, we're reminded that legacy is not only about what we build but about who gets to build in the first place. Entrepreneurial learning is not limited to formal titles or flashy success stories. It thrives in quiet workshops, open fields, local storefronts, side hustles, pop-up stands, and community-rooted collaborations.

The journey of learning at work is alive in more places than we might expect, and it shows up differently depending on lived experience, industry context, resource access, and cultural traditions. It is resilient. It is creative. And it is deeply human.

To broaden our lens and ground these ideas in real-world diversity, we now turn to the ventures and voices that often remain underrepresented in mainstream entrepreneurship conversations. In this final chapter, we explore how learning shows up in trades-based ventures, creative and cultural sectors, rural communities, immigrant-led businesses, micro-enterprises, and next-generation efforts sparked at kitchen tables and from homes with a laptop and stable Wi-Fi. These stories remind us: Legacy is already in motion. We just have to learn to see it, and support it, wherever it begins.

Every business is a legacy in the making. But legacy is not just about scale or succession but about what kind of learning we pass on, and how we grow others through our own growth. In every story we've explored, the same question echoes: How do we pass learning forward, not just within teams but across generations and communities? In this final chapter, we expand the lens to see entrepreneurial learning in new contexts, outside the mainstream, but rich in wisdom. We zoom out to explore learning across industries, life stages, and overlooked entrepreneurial communities.

This chapter intentionally takes a different form. While the earlier chapters follow a consistent structure of concepts, tools, and founder spotlights, Chapter 10 serves as the capstone, an integrative reflection on learning, legacy, and community. Because legacy is fluid, relational, and deeply personal, this chapter uses a more narrative, blended structure to invite readers into a wider lens on entrepreneurial learning. It is meant to feel expansive, reflective, and connective, closing the book by highlighting how learning extends beyond ventures and into communities, generations, and ecosystems.

CHAPTER 11

Learning in Unexpected Places: Diverse Voices of Entrepreneurial Growth

Turning Point Opening Narrative: When Innovation Looks Like Your Neighbor

When Alia opened her home-based tailoring business in a quiet suburban neighborhood, she didn't see herself as an entrepreneur. She was a newcomer to Canada, a mother of two, and a skilled seamstress trying to make ends meet. Clients came by word of mouth, someone needed a wedding sari altered, a suit adjusted, a school uniform mended.

At first, it felt like survival work. But one day, a client asked if she could teach a small sewing class for teens. Then another asked about commissioning custom designs. Then came a local boutique, interested in her pieces.

Without a website, investors, or a business degree, Alia built a sustainable, values-driven enterprise rooted in skill, trust, and community. What she lacked in formal start-up experience, she made up for with adaptability, intuition, and quiet leadership.

Alia's story reminds us that entrepreneurial learning doesn't only live in accelerators or tech hubs. It unfolds in kitchens, mobile workshops, basements, and back roads. It thrives in trades and crafts, in art and performance, in overlooked sectors and underrepresented communities. These are the stories we often forget when we talk about innovation, but they're at the heart of how our economy, culture, and communities grow.

Core Concepts: Expanding the Map
of Entrepreneurial Learning

1. **Entrepreneurship Beyond the "Start-Up" Label**
   Innovation isn't limited to venture-backed start-ups. Microbusinesses, side hustles, community enterprises, and skilled tradespeople all contribute to the entrepreneurial ecosystem. Their learning may be informal, self-guided, and embedded in practice, but it is no less strategic.
   Insight: When we broaden our definition of entrepreneurship, we expand who gets to be seen as a leader.

2. **Rural and Remote Learning Realities**
   Entrepreneurs in rural or remote areas often rely on peer networks, informal mentorship, and cross-sector partnerships to navigate business growth. Their learning tends to be hands-on and community-integrated, reflecting local priorities.
   Example: A northern food co-op that began as a seasonal market but grew into a year-round supplier by coordinating transport with a local school board.

3. **Trades-Based and Craft Sector Innovation**
   Electricians, bakers, hairstylists, and woodworkers engage in deep, embodied learning. They build knowledge through doing, mentoring, and adapting to client needs. Their ventures often become intergenerational learning hubs.
   Example: A third-generation welder who mentors young apprentices in both skill and business acumen while exploring green energy retrofits.

4. **Immigrant and Newcomer Entrepreneurship**
   Many newcomers turn to entrepreneurship out of necessity, but with creativity, resilience, and cultural intelligence, they turn these ventures into thriving businesses. Their learning is shaped by both their past experiences and the local contexts they enter.
   Example: A newcomer and extended family who turned home baking into a catering business, using Instagram to navigate a new market and expand across communities.

5. **Creative Sector Entrepreneurs**

   Artists, performers, and designers are often excluded from mainstream entrepreneurship discourse. Yet they innovate constantly, shaping new revenue models, collaborating across disciplines, and experimenting with identity, audience, and brand.

   Example: A dancer who created an inclusive performance space doubling as a wellness studio, merging cultural storytelling with sustainable business practice.

Founder Spotlights

Trades Sector—Jared, Master Plumber and Mentor

After 20 years in the trades, Jared opened his own plumbing company focused on mentorship. Apprentices rotate through both residential and commercial jobs, while also learning customer communication and invoicing systems. Jared's approach emphasizes whole-business learning, not just skill acquisition but leadership, ethics, and entrepreneurial thinking.

> *"You're not just learning pipes, you're learning how to build trust in someone's home."*

Remote and Indigenous Entrepreneur—Nikita, Eco-Tourism Guide

Based in Northern Ontario, Nikita blends Indigenous knowledge, land stewardship, and tourism. She designed a hybrid business offering guided nature experiences, cultural education, and online workshops. Her learning journey includes oral history, grant-writing, community partnerships, and digital platform development.

> *"I had to learn the language of entrepreneurship, but I never lost the language of the land."*

Newcomer and Side Hustle Story—Manuel, Mobile Bicycle Repair

A former mechanical engineer, Manuel struggled to find full-time work in his field. While working retail, he began fixing bikes from his garage. Today, his mobile repair service operates on a flexible schedule, using WhatsApp and QR-coded business cards to reach local customers. His biggest learning curve? Pricing his time.

"I knew how to fix the bikes. I had to learn how to value the service."

Creative Sector—Sangita, Cultural Stitchery Artist

Sangita began embroidering her grandmother's patterns as a form of grief healing. Friends encouraged her to share the work online. One pop-up market later, she was commissioned to create wedding gifts, wall pieces, and even album covers. She now runs workshops on heritage crafts and identity through art.

"My business grew when I realized storytelling was part of the product."

Visual Tool: The Hidden Learning Landscape Map

Use this tool to reflect on where entrepreneurial learning is happening outside the spotlight, and where it's being overlooked (Table 11.1).

Talk About It with Your Team

Use these questions to foster rich team discussions that translate individual perspectives into stronger collaboration, leadership, and growth.

- Where is entrepreneurial learning happening in your community that often goes unseen?
- What kind of knowledge do you hold that wasn't learned in a classroom, but shaped your growth?

Table 11.1 The hidden learning landscape

Learning landscape	Common features	Hidden strengths	What support could amplify it?
Rural Ventures	Resourceful, relationship-based	Cross-functional knowledge, seasonal agility	Digital access, flexible funding
Trades and Crafts	Mentor–apprentice model	Embodied learning, community loyalty	Business training, intergenerational succession tools
Newcomer Entrepreneurs	Informal, necessity-based	Cultural bridging, multilingualism	Microloans, local market training
Creative Sector	Portfolio-based, gig economy	Identity-driven branding, agility	Financial literacy, grant access
Microbusiness Owners	Self-taught, lean operations	Deep customer intimacy	Peer networks, mental health support

- Are there local entrepreneurs who wouldn't call themselves "entrepreneurs" but clearly lead, adapt, and grow ventures?
- How can we make room in our systems to *see and support* these diverse learning paths?

Chapter Close and Transition

"Entrepreneurship is a mirror of society, and society is more diverse than we imagine."

When we talk about learning at work, we must expand the frame. Tradespeople, artists, immigrants, youth, and rural innovators are all building ventures, and learning deeply as they do. By spotlighting these paths, we don't just tell better stories. We build a more inclusive future of entrepreneurship. What are you building, and what are you learning, through the everyday act of showing up, trying, and evolving?

Conclusion: The Venture as a Living System

Turning Point Opening Narrative: What We Learn from the Way We Build

A business owner once told her team, "Our company isn't just a product. It's a living system that reflects how we grow, how we learn, and how we lead." Ten years in, her venture had changed form many times, new markets, new teammates, new purpose. But what remained consistent was how they made decisions: reflectively, inclusively, and with integrity.

Their growth was not measured only in revenue. It was measured in resilience, reputation, and renewal. When the economy shifted, they adapted. When people left, they invested in those who stayed. When mistakes happened, they reflected together, learning not just how to fix problems but how to build better systems for the future.

This is the essence of a venture as a living system. Businesses are not static. They breathe, evolve, and mirror the choices of their leaders.

Core Concepts: Why Ventures Must Be Seen as Living Systems

The Venture as a Reflection of Its Founders

How you build is how you lead. And how you lead shapes who you become. Each chapter of this book has shown that ventures and small businesses reflect the inner worlds of their founders, purpose, fears, values, and growth edges.

Living Systems Thrive Through Learning

Healthy ventures, like ecosystems, adapt because they learn. They take in feedback, notice patterns, and adjust. When reflection is embedded in the system—not just left to chance—businesses become more resilient.

From Founder Identity to Shared Purpose

At first, ventures often mirror a single founder's identity. But sustainability requires a shift from "my vision" to "our purpose." The strongest businesses become collective stories, not solo hustles.

Integration of Practice, Pedagogy, and Purpose

The heart of this book has been the three anchors, Practice, Pedagogy, Purpose. When applied together, they form the DNA of learning-centered leadership: concrete actions, learning processes, and values-based direction.

Sustainable Growth

The future of work demands growth that balances reflection, connection, and experimentation. Scale is not sustainable if people are left behind. True growth is measured not just in numbers but in the capacity to keep adapting with integrity.

> *"You're not late. You're not behind. You're building on your own timeline, and that matters."*

Founder Spotlight: What Kind of Venture Leader Are You Becoming?

Across this book, we've met founders who faced failure, reinvention, resistance, and growth. Some lost their way and found it again. Some passed the torch to the next generation. Some shifted identities entirely, building new lives after burnout or exits.

The common thread? They didn't lead with perfect answers. They led by asking better questions. They didn't build alone, but invited others into the learning. Their ventures became living reflections of their own transformation.

So the final question this book leaves you with is not just, "What kind of business are you building?" but, "What kind of leader are you becoming?"

Visual Tool: The Leadership Integration Canvas

Use this canvas to reflect on your journey and map what's next (Table C.1).

Table C.1 The leadership integration Canvas

Reflection prompt	Why it matters	Your notes
What have you learned about yourself through building this venture?	Awareness anchors future choices.	
What practices keep you grounded and growing?	Sustainable routines protect your energy.	
How are you designing learning into your next chapter?	Learning systems future-proof ventures.	
What's your evolving purpose, and who are you becoming as a leader?	Identity evolves; clarity strengthens influence.	

How to Use It:

- As a closing exercise for yourself, your team, or at an annual retreat.
- Capture not just what you've done but what you've become.
- Revisit yearly to see how your leadership identity evolves.

Talk About It with Your Team

Bring the journey full circle with these questions:

- What have we learned together in the past year?
- How is our business growing us, not just the other way around?
- What will it take to keep leading with courage, reflection, and care?

Personas Revisited: Whom This Book Is For

As you reflect, return to the personas who guided this book. They represent not only fictional composites but real patterns we've seen in entrepreneurs today:

- **The Purpose-Driven Founder**—striving to keep values at the center while scaling.

- **The Builder-Coach**—learning to pass the torch and grow entrepreneurs from within.
- **The Emerging People Leader**—navigating burnout and unclear pathways with a human-first approach.
- **The Reflective Entrepreneurial Educator**—equipping others with tools for intentional leadership.
- **The Social Entrepreneur/Maker-Founder**—scaling without selling out, weaving life, work, and community together.

These personas echo the book's audience: entrepreneurs like you who are not just asking, "How do I scale?" but, "How do I grow people while I grow the business? How do I make this venture reflect my values? How can I lead in a way that feels human and sustainable?"

Chapter Close and Transition

Entrepreneurial Learning at Work has been an invitation. To rethink entrepreneurship not as hustle but as a relational, reflective practice. To see ventures not as static companies but as living systems shaped by choices, values, and learning.

In today's global, rapidly changing world, this mindset is not optional. It is what sustains ventures through complexity. It is what creates cultures people want to join. It is what allows entrepreneurs to grow with integrity.

So as you close this book, the final question is yours: "Your business is not just what you do. It's how you choose to grow." What kind of leader, and what kind of system, are you choosing to build?

Appendixes: Ancillary Tools and Resources

Appendix A: For Those Learning While Building

Not all beginnings feel like a clean slate. Sometimes, they come after a pause. After burnout. After loss, reinvention, transition. Sometimes, they come mid-sentence, while you're still running a business, raising a family, or working a day job that funds the dream.

This book is for you too.

For the builder returning to something they once loved.
For the tradesperson learning new tools in a digitized world.
For the community-rooted entrepreneur reshaping a practice in a changing economy.
For the teacher-turned-coach, the contractor now consulting, the designer who's found their way back to making.

Whether you're starting something new or adapting what you've already built, your work matters. This isn't just a guide for the early stage or the start-up sprint. It's for the long game. For building with care. For staying in motion. For reimagining what your work can become.

You don't have to have it all figured out. You don't need perfect timing or perfect confidence.
You just need to keep going, with intention, with reflection, and with people beside you who believe in your vision.

You are not behind. You are not alone.
You are not too late. You are not too small.
You are right on time.

Keep building. We need what only you can create. Some of the strongest foundations are built in the middle of change.

Appendix B—Mapping the Journey of Entrepreneurial Learning

This appendix offers a visual summary of the core practices explored throughout the book. It is designed as a reference and reflection tool to help readers connect the six learning practices to their own entrepreneurial journey, whether at the stage of starting up, growing a team, or rethinking what comes next.

The table below maps each practice across stages of venture development, links them to real-world examples from founder profiles, and suggests tools or reflection prompts to guide further action. Whether you're a first-time founder, a seasoned entrepreneur facing change, or someone guiding others through the venture-building process, this overview can help you locate where you are, and where to go next.

This summary table reinforces the six core practices of entrepreneurial learning introduced throughout the book. It illustrates how each practice applies across key business stages and references where readers can find related stories, founder profiles, and tools (Table A.1).

Table A.1 Mapping the journey of entrepreneurial learning

Practice	Application across stages	Chapters and stories	Tools and reflections
1. Identity in Action	Clarifying personal values and leadership identity as the foundation of the venture	Chapter 2 (Beyond the Start-Up Myth) Chapter 3 (The Entrepreneur as Learner)	Entrepreneur's Reflection Cycle
2. Embedded Learning Systems	Creating day-to-day mechanisms for continuous learning, feedback, and growth	Chapter 4 (Structuring Learning into Daily Work) Chapter 5 (Growing Talent from Within)	Learning Map Culture Reflection Tool
3. People Development as Strategy	Integrating talent growth, mentorship, and team learning into the business model	Chapter 6 (Culture Is Your Competitive Advantage) Chapter 7 (Navigating Change with a Human Lens)	Entrepreneurial Talent Fit Canvas

Practice	Application across stages	Chapters and stories	Tools and reflections
4. Leading Human-Centered Change	Responding to internal and external change with empathy, clarity, and purpose	Chapter 8 (Making Learning Visible and Scalable) Chapter 9 (Designing for the Future of Work)	Leading Through Change Conversation Guide
5. Scalable Learning	Using systems, roles, and partnerships to spread learning across growing ventures	Chapter 10 (Your Learning Legacy) Chapter 11 (Learning in Unexpected Places)	Learning Ecosystem Map
6. Reflective Narrative Practice	Capturing and sharing stories as a means to learn, grow, and lead with intention	Chapter 11 (Learning in Unexpected Places) Founder Spotlights throughout	Story Audit Worksheet Legacy Conversation Starters

What We Mean When We Say …

Entrepreneurial Learning

More than just gaining business skills, entrepreneurial learning is the ongoing process of making sense of challenges, adapting to change, and applying insight to lead your business forward. It happens through reflection, feedback, decisions, and doing, not just training.

Embedded Coaching

The practice of weaving developmental support (like mentoring, feedback, or growth conversations) into daily business activities. Instead of pulling people out for training, you grow them inside the flow of work.

Leadership Integration

Bringing together different parts of yourself, your values, experiences, knowledge, and relationships, into how you lead every day. It's about showing up with integrity, not switching hats between "leader" and "person."

Learning-in-Action

Learning that happens not in theory but in the middle of doing the work—it's messy, fast, often uncomfortable, but essential. Entrepreneurs don't wait for perfect clarity; they learn as they go.

Learning Culture

A work environment where curiosity, questions, and mistakes are part of the process. It's about creating space for people to develop, adapt, and grow as your business evolves.

The Life Course

A perspective that recognizes that people (including entrepreneurs) move through different stages in life, each with its own needs, risks, and motivations. It reminds us that how we learn, lead, and build shifts over time.

Living Systems

A way of understanding your business as a dynamic, evolving system made up of people, processes, and purpose. Like any living system, your venture needs attention to growth, adaptation, energy, and connection to its environment. It's not just a machine; it's something that breathes.

People-Centered Leadership

Leading in a way that puts people—not just productivity—at the heart of your decisions. It includes empathy, inclusion, respect, and building cultures where people feel seen and valued.

Practice, Pedagogy, Purpose

A three-part lens that runs through this book:

- Practice is what you do.
- Pedagogy is how you and others learn.
- Purpose is why it matters.

Together, they shape how you build your venture and develop your team.

Reflective Practice

The habit of pausing to ask: What just happened? What does it mean? What might I do differently next time? Reflective practice turns experience into insight and helps entrepreneurs lead with intention.

Scalable Learning

The ability to build systems, habits, and mindsets in your business that allow everyone—not just the founder—to learn and adapt as the business grows.

Systems Thinking

Seeing the bigger picture: how different parts of your business connect and influence each other. It helps you make better decisions, spot unintended consequences, and lead change more effectively.

Talent as Growth Engine

Instead of just viewing staff as roles to fill, this means developing your people as your competitive advantage. Talent, when nurtured, becomes a source of innovation, energy, and long-term business growth.

Work-Integrated Learning (WIL)

Real-world experiences (such as internships, co-ops, or project placements) where students learn through doing. For entrepreneurs, WIL creates a valuable bridge between your business and emerging talent pipelines.

References

AndeGlobal. *What We Know About Talent Management.* Aspen Network of Development Entrepreneurs, 2021.

Argyris, Chris, and Donald A. Schön. *Organizational Learning II: Theory, Method, and Practice.* Addison-Wesley, 1996.

Association for Talent Development. *ATD Research: Informal Learning Offers Flexibility in Skills Development.* ATD Press, 2024. https://www.td.org/content/press-release/atd-research-informal-learning-offers-flexibility-in-skills-development.

Bovell, Sinead. "Sinead Bovell." *Wikipedia,* last modified August 30, 2025. https://en.wikipedia.org/wiki/Sinead_Bovell.

Bregman, Rutger. *Moral Ambition: Stop Wasting Your Talent and Start Making a Difference.* London: Bloomsbury Publishing, 2025.

Business Insider. "Gen Z Is Avoiding Management Roles to Protect Their Mental Health." *Business Insider,* April 2025.

Cope, Matt. "Entrepreneurial Learning from Failure: An Interpretative Phenomenological Analysis." *Journal of Business Venturing* 26, no. 6 (2011): 604–23.

Corley, Constance Saltz, and Karen Miller. "Lifelong Learning and Life History: A Life Course Perspective." Paper prepared for the Gerontological Society of America Conference, Orlando, FL, 2005. Fielding Graduate University, 2005.

Cowan Sahadath, Kathy. "Visionary and Entrepreneurial Thinking: A Life Course Approach." Master's thesis, Fielding Graduate University, 2009.

Deloitte. *Gen Z and Millennial Survey.* Deloitte Insights, 2025.

Edmondson, Amy C. *The Fearless Organization: Creating Psychological Safety in the Workplace for Learning, Innovation, and Growth.* Wiley, 2019.

Fayolle, Alain. *A Research Agenda for Entrepreneurial Learning.* Edward Elgar, 2020.

Filion, Louis Jacques, Jean-Michel Saive, and Lucie Morin. *Agents of Innovation: Entrepreneurs—Facilitators—Intrapreneurs.* Emerald Publishing, 2023.

Heijden, Helena van der, and Josette Dijkhuizen. "Feedback Culture in Entrepreneurial Teams: Toward Resilient Learning Environments." *International Small Business Journal* 39, no. 4 (2021): 367–89.

International Labour Organization. *Creating a Conducive Environment for Women's Entrepreneurship Development.* International Labour Organization, 2023.

Irene, Bridget, Eunice Oluwakem Chukwuma-Nwuba, Joan Lockyer, Chioma Onoshakpor, and Siona Ndeh. "Entrepreneurial Learning in Informal

Apprenticeship Programs: Exploring the Learning Process of the Igbo Apprenticeship System in Nigeria." *Cogent Business & Management* 11, no. 1 (2024): 2399312..

Katsaros, Konstantinos K. "Gen Z Employee Adaptive Performance: The Role of Inclusive Leadership." *Administrative Sciences* 14, no. 8 (2024): 163. https://doi.org/10.3390/admsci14080163.

Kolb, David A. *Experiential Learning: Experience as the Source of Learning and Development.* 2nd ed. Pearson, 2015.

London, Manuel, and James W. Smither. "Feedback Orientation and Feedback Culture: Opportunities for Learning." *Human Resource Development Review* 19, no. 1 (2020): 20–47.

MaRS Discovery District. *Virtual Entrepreneurship: How Canadian Digital Support Programs Transform Business Success.* MaRS, 2023. https://www.industryandbusiness.ca/virtual-entrepreneurship-how-canadian-digital-support-programs-transform-business-success/.

Marsick, Victoria J., and Karen E. Watkins. *Informal and Incidental Learning in the Workplace.* 2nd ed. Routledge, 2018.

McKinsey Global Institute. *A New Future of Work: The Race to Deploy AI and Raise Skills in Europe and Beyond.* McKinsey & Company, May 2024.

Organisation for Economic Co-operation and Development (OECD). *SME and Entrepreneurship Outlook 2023.* OECD Publishing, 2023. https://www.oecd.org/en/publications/2023/06/oecd-sme-and-entrepreneurship-outlook-2023_c5ac21d0.html.

Rae, David. "Entrepreneurial Learning: Conceptual Frameworks and Applications." *Technovation* 26, no. 3 (2006): 307–18.

Shepherd, Dean A., and Holger Patzelt. *Learning from Entrepreneurial Failure.* Cambridge University Press, 2018.

Singh, Satwinder, and Andrea Gibbs. "Entrepreneurship across the Life Course: Developmental Pathways and Identity Shifts." *Entrepreneurship Theory and Practice* 45, no. 6 (2021): 1335–58.

Souza, Marcus Vinícius de, and Matthew S. Wood. "Adaptive Learning in Entrepreneurial Contexts: Navigating Complexity Through Sensemaking." *International Journal of Entrepreneurial Behavior and Research* 28, no. 6 (2022): 1403–21.

St-Jean, Étienne, and Mathieu Tremblay. "Mentorship for Novice Entrepreneurs: Learning and Sensemaking in Practice." *Journal of Small Business Management* 58, no. 1 (2020): 94–122.

Susskind, Daniel. *Growth: A Reckoning.* PublicAffairs, 2024.

Uhl-Bien, Mary, and Russ Marion. "Complexity Leadership in Action: A Hybrid Approach for Adaptive Change." *Organizational Dynamics* 50, no. 2 (2021): 1–10.

About the Author

Dr. Kathy Cowan Sahadath is an accomplished business leader, educator, and author with more than 30 years of experience in strategic project and change management, organizational development, and leadership transformation. She has held senior roles across complex, multistakeholder organizations, leading large-scale change initiatives, building inclusive talent pipelines, and advising executive teams on navigating workforce disruption, digital transformation, and strategic alignment.

Kathy Cowan Sahadath is a leadership strategist, educator, and researcher focused on entrepreneurial learning and people-centered venture design. Her work blends systems thinking with practical insight to help founders and curious leaders grow their businesses through culture, reflection, and adaptive leadership.

Kathy has spent over two decades advising founders, small business owners, and project-based leaders across sectors. She teaches in the areas of entrepreneurship, organizational change, and leadership development, bringing a practice-based approach grounded in adult learning and storytelling. Since 2020, she has written 27 novels exploring themes of entrepreneurship, identity, and resilience—narratives that mirror the lived experience of entrepreneurial growth.

Her current research and teaching explore how entrepreneurial learning happens in real time, through feedback, reflection, and the everyday challenges of building something that matters.

Her academic credentials include an undergraduate degree in psychology, an MBA in project management, an MA in human and organizational development, and a PhD in human and organizational systems, where her research focused on how senior leaders use conversation to shape and sustain organizational change. She has also taught extensively in postsecondary institutions, combining adult learning theory, inclusive pedagogy, and outcome-based design to foster reflective leadership and systems thinking across professional and educational settings.

Kathy's ability to integrate practical leadership expertise with academic insight is matched by her commitment to storytelling as a learning and leadership tool. Since 2020, she has written 26 novels exploring themes of entrepreneurship and leadership, identity, resilience, and human connection, stories that resonate deeply with adult readers and reflect the emotional landscape of modern work and life. This narrative lens enriches her ability to design inclusive, human-centered learning experiences and to speak across disciplines and generations.

As a consultant and facilitator, she continues to support organizations and educational institutions in aligning business strategy with organizational change, particularly in areas such as inclusive governance, change communication, and academic innovation, A professor at various higher educational institutions teaching curriculum, for example, Entrepreneurship and Small Business, Business Management Fundamentals, Leading Strategic Change and a Digital Transformation series. Passionate about helping students and entrepreneurs develop their unique brands and innovative business models.

Her writing bridges business practice, research, and creative insight, making her uniquely positioned to contribute to the evolving discourse on leadership, project transformation, and organizational change.

Index

www.ingramcontent.com/pod-product-compliance
Lightning Source LLC
Chambersburg PA
CBHW071013200526
45171CB00007B/124